Battlegroun

The Canal Line

Battleground series:

Stamford Bridge & Hastings *by* Peter Marren
Wars of the Roses - Wakefield/ Towton by Philip A. Haigh
Wars of the Roses - Barnet by David Clark
Wars of the Roses - Tewkesbury by Steven Goodchild
Wars of the Roses - The Battles of St Albans by
Peter Burley, Michael Elliott & Harvey Wilson
English Civil War - Naseby by Martin Marix Evans, Peter Burton
and Michael Westaway
English Civil War - Marston Moor by David Clark
War of the Spanish Succession - Blenheim 1704 by James Falkner
War of the Spanish Succession - Ramillies 1706 by James Falkner
Napoleonic - Hougoumont by Julian Paget and Derek Saunders
Napoleonic - Waterloo by Andrew Uffindell and Michael Corum
Zulu War - Isandlwana by Ian Knight and Ian Castle
Zulu War - Rorkes Drift by Ian Knight and Ian Castle
Boer War - The Relief of Ladysmith by Lewis Childs
Boer War - The Siege of Ladysmith by Lewis Childs
Boer War - Kimberley by Lewis Childs

Mons *by* Jack Horsfall and Nigel Cave
Néry *by* Patrick Tackle
Retreat of I Corps 1914 *by* Jerry Murland
Aisne 1914 *by* Jerry Murland
Aisne 1918 *by* David Blanchard
Le Cateau *by* Nigel Cave and Jack Shelden
Walking the Salient *by* Paul Reed
Ypres - 1914 Messines by Nigel Cave and Jack Sheldon
Ypres - 1914 Menin Road by Nigel Cave and Jack Sheldon
Ypres - 1914 Langemarck by Jack Sheldonand Nigel Cave
Ypres - Sanctuary Wood and Hooge by Nigel Cave
Ypres - Hill 60 by Nigel Cave
Ypres - Messines Ridge by Peter Oldham
Ypres - Polygon Wood by Nigel Cave
Ypres - Passchendaele by Nigel Cave
Ypres - Airfields and Airmen by Mike O'Connor
Ypres - St Julien by Graham Keech
Ypres - Boesinghe by Stephen McGreal
Walking the Somme *by* Paul Reed
Somme - Gommecourt by Nigel Cave
Somme - Serre by Jack Horsfall & Nigel Cave
Somme - Beaumont Hamel by Nigel Cave
Somme - Thiepval by Michael Stedman
Somme - La Boisselle by Michael Stedman
Somme - Fricourt by Michael Stedman
Somme - Carnoy-Montauban by Graham Maddocks
Somme - Pozières by Graham Keech
Somme - Courcelette by Paul Reed
Somme - Boom Ravine by Trevor Pidgeon
Somme - Mametz Wood by Michael Renshaw
Somme - Delville Wood by Nigel Cave
Somme - Advance to Victory (North) 1918 by Michael Stedman
Somme - Flers by Trevor Pidgeon
Somme - Bazentin Ridge by Edward Hancock
Somme - Combles by Paul Reed
Somme - Beaucourt by Michael Renshaw
Somme - Redan Ridge by Michael Renshaw
Somme - Hamel by Peter Pedersen
Somme - Villers-Bretonneux by Peter Pedersen
Somme - Airfields and Airmen by Mike O'Connor
Airfields and Airmen of the Channel Coast *by* Mike O'Connor
In the Footsteps of the Red Baron *by* Mike O'Connor
Arras - Airfields and Airmen by Mike O'Connor
Arras - The Battle for Vimy Ridge by Jack Sheldon & Nigel Cave
Arras - Vimy Ridge by Nigel Cave
Arras - Gavrelle by Trevor Tasker and Kyle Tallett
Arras - Oppy Wood by David Bilton
Arras - Bullecourt by Graham Keech
Arras - Monchy le Preux by Colin Fox
Walking Arras *by* Paul Reed
Hindenburg Line *by* Peter Oldham
Hindenburg Line - Epehy by Bill Mitchinson
Hindenburg Line - Riqueval by Bill Mitchinson
Hindenburg Line - Villers-Plouich by Bill Mitchinson
Hindenburg Line - Cambrai Right Hook by Jack Horsfall & Nigel Cave
Hindenburg Line - Cambrai Flesquières by Jack Horsfall & Nigel Cave
Hindenburg Line - Saint Quentin by Helen McPhail and Philip Guest
Hindenburg Line - Bourlon Wood by Jack Horsfall & Nigel Cave

Cambrai - Airfields and Airmen by Mike O'Connor
Aubers Ridge *by* Edward Hancock
La Bassée - Neuve Chapelle by Geoffrey Bridger
Loos - Hohenzollern Redoubt by Andrew Rawson
Loos - Hill 70 by Andrew Rawson
Fromelles *by* Peter Pedersen
The Battle of the Lys 1918 *by* Phil Tomaselli
Accrington Pals Trail *by* William Turner
Poets at War: Wilfred Owen *by* Helen McPhail and Philip Guest
Poets at War: Edmund Blunden *by* Helen McPhail and Philip Guest
Poets at War: Graves & Sassoon *by* Helen McPhail and Philip Guest
Gallipoli *by* Nigel Steel
Gallipoli - Gully Ravine by Stephen Chambers
Gallipoli - Anzac Landing by Stephen Chambers
Gallipoli - Suvla August Offensive by Stephen Chambers
Gallipoli - Landings at Helles by Huw & Jill Rodge
Walking the Gallipoli *by* Stephen Chambers
Walking the Italian Front *by* Francis Mackay
Italy - Asiago by Francis Mackay
Verdun: Fort Douamont by Christina Holstein
Verdun: Fort Vaux by Christina Holstein
Walking Verdun *by* Christina Holstein
Verdun: The Left Bank by Christina Holstein
Zeebrugge & Ostend Raids 1918 by Stephen McGreal

Germans at Beaumont Hamel *by* Jack Sheldon
Germans at Thiepval *by* Jack Sheldon

SECOND WORLD WAR

Dunkirk *by* Patrick Wilson
Calais *by* Jon Cooksey
Boulogne *by* Jon Cooksey
Saint-Nazaire *by* James Dorrian
Walking D-Day *by* Paul Reed
Atlantic Wall - Pas de Calais by Paul Williams
Atlantic Wall - Normandy by Paul Williams
Normandy - Pegasus Bridge by Carl Shilleto
Normandy - Merville Battery by Carl Shilleto
Normandy - Utah Beach by Carl Shilleto
Normandy - Omaha Beach by Tim Kilvert-Jones
Normandy - Gold Beach by Christopher Dunphie & Garry Johnson
Normandy - Gold Beach Jig by Tim Saunders
Normandy - Juno Beach by Tim Saunders
Normandy - Sword Beach by Tim Kilvert-Jones
Normandy - Operation Bluecoat by Ian Daglish
Normandy - Operation Goodwood by Ian Daglish
Normandy - Epsom by Tim Saunders
Normandy - Hill 112 by Tim Saunders
Normandy - Mont Pinçon by Eric Hunt
Normandy - Cherbourg by Andrew Rawson
Normandy - Commandos & Rangers on D-Day by Tim Saunders
Das Reich – Drive to Normandy by Philip Vickers
Oradour *by* Philip Beck
Market Garden - Nijmegen by Tim Saunders
Market Garden - Hell's Highway by Tim Saunders
Market Garden - Arnhem, Oosterbeek by Frank Steer
Market Garden - Arnhem, The Bridge by Frank Steer
Market Garden - The Island by Tim Saunders
Rhine Crossing – US 9th Army & 17th US Airborne by Andrew Rawson
British Rhine Crossing – Operation Varsity by Tim Saunders
British Rhine Crossing – Operation Plunder by Tim Saunders
Battle of the Bulge – St Vith by Michael Tolhurst
Battle of the Bulge – Bastogne by Michael Tolhurst
Channel Islands *by* George Forty
Walcheren *by* Andrew Rawson
Remagen Bridge *by* Andrew Rawson
Cassino *by* Ian Blackwell
Anzio *by* Ian Blackwell
Dieppe *by* Tim Saunders
Fort Eben Emael *by* Tim Saunders
Crete – The Airborne Invasion by Tim Saunders
Malta *by* Paul Williams
Bruneval Raid *by* Paul Oldfield
Cockleshell Raid *by* Paul Oldfield

Battleground Europe

The Canal Line

France and Flanders Campaign
1940

Jerry Murland

Series Editor
Nigel Cave

Pen & Sword
MILITARY

First published in Great Britain in 2018 by
Pen & Sword Military
An imprint of
Pen & Sword Books Ltd
47 Church Street
Barnsley
South Yorkshire
S70 2AS

ISBN 978 147385 219 8

A CIP catalogue record for this book is
available from the British Library.

Typeset in Times New Roman by Chic Graphics

Printed and bound in England by
CPI Group (UK) Ltd., Croydon, CR0 4YY

Pen & Sword Books Ltd incorporates the imprints of
Pen & Sword Archaeology, Atlas, Aviation, Battleground, Discovery,
Family History, History, Maritime, Military, Naval, Politics,
Railways, Select, Social History, Transport, True Crime,
Claymore Press, Frontline Books, Leo Cooper, Praetorian Press,
Remember When, Seaforth Publishing and Wharncliffe.

For a complete list of Pen & Sword titles please contact
PEN & SWORD BOOKS LIMITED
47 Church Street, Barnsley, South Yorkshire, S70 2AS, England
E-mail: enquiries@pen-and-sword.co.uk
Website: www.pen-and-sword.co.uk

Contents

List of Maps

Introduction by Series Editor

It was sheer coincidence when I got the proof for this book, the fourth in Jerry Murland's France and Flanders 1940 set of Battleground Europe books, that I also happened to be proofing Chris Baker's book in the same series, *The Battle of the Lys 1918: Objective Hazebrouck*. I found myself reading about actions that were often taking place over much the same ground, with the BEF of 1914-18 on the back foot in April 1918 against a major German offensive, just as its successor found itself in late May 1940 but with a much less happy outcome. Some who fought in 1940 were there twenty two years earlier; whilst large numbers, as Jerry points out, would have been the sons of those who had battled, in their case successfully, to halt that German desperate attempt to bring the First World War to a satisfactory conclusion.

As for so much of the campaign in May and June 1940, the book records the heroic attempts by members of the BEF, often supported by French troops, to hold back the Germans from the Dunkirk perimeter, where a limited evacuation had already taken place and where the main evacuation got under way on 26 May. The defenders had to face great odds – not only the might of the German forces brought to bear on them but also considerable confusion of command: the always difficult relationship between allied armies, each operating under different political imperatives; the problem of fighting a succession of rear guard actions; hazy information about the tactical situation, made much worse by poor communications; units often thrown into action inadequately equipped; and receiving conflicting orders. The men on the ground had to make the best of a bad job, as flanks gave way, positions were over-run, encirclement threatened.

For a variety of reasons, including the still controversial reasoning behind Hitler's Halt Order of 24 May (how significant the role of von Rundstedt was in this is still argued by military historians), the BEF and associated French forces bought enough time to make the perimeter as secure as possible and the outcome entered popular myth. In reality a catastrophe had been averted, but a military disaster it certainly was. Such was the skill of the contemporary 'spin doctors' that the unlikely outcome of this disaster was that it served to unite the British people, possibly helped by the fact that civilians and their 'small boats' played a notable part in it. The 'Dunkirk Spirit' entered and remains in the popular lexicon.

There could have been no successful evacuation without the

determined, if ultimately hopeless, efforts made by the defenders of the flat lands around St-Omer. This could be a brutal campaign, as illustrated by the massacre of prisoners, mainly men from the Royal Norfolk Regiment, in the small hamlet of Le Paradis.

As for other areas covered by the series, a notable number of the fatal casualties of the BEF are to be found in small group – sometimes even individual – burials in the cemeteries of the communes in the area, often sharing the same part of the cemetery as their predecessors of 1918. Jerry's narrative will encourage more of us to stop for a few minutes to pay tribute to the memory of so many unsung heroes in such a desperate period of the nation's history.

Nigel Cave
Ratcliffe College, 2018

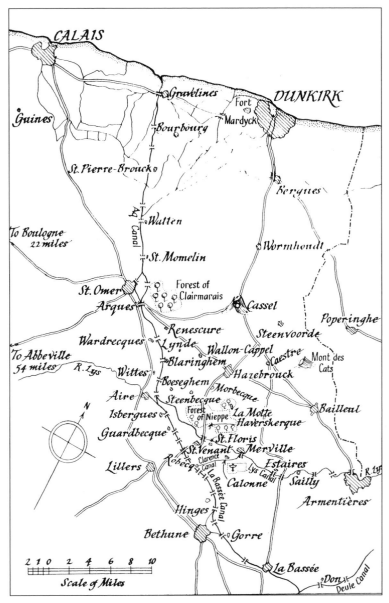

The Canal Line ran from Gravelines in the north to the Deûle Canal in the south east.

Author's Introduction

Introduction

The network of canals stretching from the coast at Gravelines, through St-Omer, Béthune and La Bassée, follows the approximate boundary between Artois and Flanders and was, in 1940, the defensive line established on the western and southern edges of the so-called Dunkerque corridor designed by Gort to provide an evacuation route to the channel coast.

Early History

Four of the towns situated along the canal, Gravelines, Aire-sur-la-Lys, St-Venant and Béthune, had been fortified by Sébastien Vauban (1633-1707) and were amongst the towns that Marlborough had found necessary to capture in 1710 as a preliminary to his campaign of 1711. The small coastal town of Gravelines has, like its larger neighbour Dunkerque, a long history as a North Sea fishing port. After Louis XIV captured the northern borderlands of France, Vauban was directed to strengthen the town's fortifications with his characteristic, and extremely effective, star-shaped defences. Prior to this, the town grew in importance during the early 12th century when silting of the waterways gradually cut St-Omer off from the North Sea, resulting in the construction of a navigable canal from St-Omer to the North Sea at Gravelines. In 1520 the Holy Roman

Place Albert Denvers at Gravelines.

X

Emperor, Charles V, and Henry VIII of England met at Gravelines and in 1588 Lord Howard launched an attack from England using fire ships against the Spanish Armada at anchor there.

Like many of the large towns along the canal, St-Omer saw its allegiance swing between the Earls of Flanders, Dukes of Burgundy and Spain, before it was finally annexed to France in the Treaty of the Pyrenees of 1659. The associations with British history include the Jesuit connection and its links with Stonyhurst College in Lancashire and, although specific evidence has never been found, it is said to be the town in which the executioner of Anne Boleyn lived and was, more than likely, the venue for the initial planning of the Gunpowder Plot of 1605. In 1783 the town was visited by the young Lieutenant Horatio Nelson with the intention of learning French. Whether much French was learned is a matter of conjecture!

Amongst its many architectural and cultural attractions, the town boasts a magnificent 13th century Gothic Cathedral, an exceptionally fine Flemish market square with a weekly Saturday market, an excellent museum – Musée de l'Hotel Sandelin – and an impressive Hôtel de Ville containing the 18th century Italianate theatre. Not only that, but there are a myriad of restaurants in the squares and streets of the old town that offer the visitor a varied and affordable menu. In more recent times the town was host to GHQ (until 1916) of the 1914-1918 BEF – a building we visit in **Walk 1** – and is still considered the spiritual home of the

The cathedral of Notre Dame in St-Omer is amongst the finest in France.

Royal Air Force through its association with the Royal Flying Corps. St-Omer was liberated on 5 September 1944 by the 1st Polish Armoured Division.

Further south the ravages of war continued to surround the towns on the canal. St-Venant was no exception and became a centre of attention in 1639 when Louis of France began his campaign of returning Artois and French Flanders to the French crown. Arras fell to the French in 1640 and, seven years later, St-Venant was finally taken by Marshal Turenne's forces. From June 1915 to October 1917, the British and Indian health services were established in St-Venant and from May 1917 until April 1918, the town became the headquarters of the Portugese Expeditionary Force.

The Polish Memorial on Rue d'Arras, St-Omer, commemorating the liberation of the town in September 1944.

The Canal

While the author has used the generic term canal to describe the waterway, there are in fact four separate sections of the canal, which in itself can be a little confusing. North of St-Omer the canal is called the Canal de l'Aa, whereas from St-Omer to Aire-sur-la-Lys the canal goes under the name, Canal de Neufossé. Aire-sur-la-Lys is also the junction with the canalized River Lys, which cuts eastwards through St-Venant towards Merville. South of Aire-sur-la-Lys the canal adopts the name Canal de l'Aire à La Bassée until it reaches the junction with the Deûle Canal at Bauvin. To confuse matters further, the Lys Canal, which was the scene of the 6 Brigade stand at St-Venant, is also referred to in some publications as the Bourne Canal.

Since May 1940 the canal has been widened in several places and the bridges replaced with modern structures capable of bearing the increased weight of traffic. Where a bridge is described in the text as being swung *open* it means that the bridge is closed to road traffic and pedestrians, but *open* to water traffic. Thus Guderian's XIX Corps would have found the swing bridges on the Canal de l'Aa *opened* by the defending garrison.

The canal south of St-Omer as it is today.

Sources

Material concerning the deployment of units along the canal in 1940 has been found in a variety of sources, including regimental histories and unit war diaries. While the war diaries give an overall picture of daily events, the reader should be aware that frequently these diaries were completed after the event and are not always entirely accurate. It is also regrettable that all too often regimental historians relied on those diaries and on information provided long after the events took place. Personal diaries are usually a little more accurate in content but are sometimes difficult to match with events that took place on a wider strategic front. However, I have been fortunate in being able to access a number of personal diaries and accounts from men serving with the independent 25 Brigade and the 2nd Division, which has, in some cases, added to and enhanced the actions taken by those units while deployed on the canal. The author has altered some personal accounts and quotes slightly to ensure they make sense and, where necessary, has added his own words, contained in square brackets, to assist the reader. With regard to the actions of the battalions of the 2nd Division, there is little doubt that they were sacrificed to enable the Canal Line to remain intact for as long as possible, although the casualties inflicted on 6 Brigade at St-Venant could possibly have been much reduced had they been allowed to position themselves north of the Lys Canal.

Casualties

Readers may wonder why the information concerning officers appears to be greater than that of the other ranks who died, often in the same engagements. The answer is quite simple: there is more information provided about officer casualties than for other ranks, particularly in battalion war diaries and regimental histories. Another question that frequently arises concerns the whereabouts of the losses reported in a specific engagement, particularly when casualties cannot be found in nearby cemeteries. Many of these soldiers either remained unidentified or even unidentifiable, which is why their names appear on the Dunkirk Memorial. A name inscribed on the memorial will often correspond to an unidentified grave somewhere in France or Belgium.

Ranks and Abbreviations

The ranks given to each individual are those that were held in May 1940 and do not reflect any subsequent promotion received by an individual unless stated; and when describing the fighting I have often referred to modern day road numbering in order to give the reader using current maps of the area a more precise location. PSM is an abbreviation of Platoon Sergeant Major, an appointment that was short-lived and carried the rank of warrant officer class III (WOIII). Created in 1938, it was designed to give NCOs experience in commanding units formally commanded by commissioned officers. No promotions to the rank were made after 1940. I have also used a form of abbreviation when describing units and formations, for example, after its first mention in the text, 9th Battalion Royal Northumberland Fusiliers becomes the 9/RNF and the 1st Battalion Royal Irish Fusiliers becomes 1/RIF. Infantry battalions were generally divided into four companies and an HQ Company that included the battalion signallers, dispatch riders and medical staff.

German army units are a little more complex. Within the infantry regiment there were three battalions – each one approximately the size of a British battalion – and again, I have abbreviated when describing these units, thus the 73rd Infantry Regiment becomes IR73, while the second battalion within that regiment is abbreviated to II/IR73; or, in the case of panzer regiments, II/Pz5. Each infantry battalion was broken down into four companies of riflemen, who were given an Arabic numeral, for example, 3 *Kompanie.*

Some of the equivalent German and British ranks referred to in the text are as follows:

Lieutenant General	*Generaloberst, General der Panzertruppe, Obergruppenführer*
Major General	*Generalmajor*
Colonel	*Oberst*
Lieutenant Colonel	*Oberstleutnant*
Major	*Major, Sturmbannführer*
Captain	*Hauptmann, Hauptsturmführer*
Lieutenant	*Oberleutnant*
Second Lieutenant	*Leutnant*
Corporal	*Unteroffizier*
Lance Corporal	*Gefreiter*
Infantry Private	*Infanterist, Schütze*

Acknowledgements

No book of this nature can be completed without the help and assistance offered by others and in this case I must acknowledge the assistance given by Tim Lynch, particularly for Brigadier John Gawthorpe's article in *Ca Ira* and Matthew Richardson, who has very kindly allowed me to use some of the interviews he conducted with former members of the Leicestershire Regiment. I would thoroughly recommend Ray Goodacre's book on the 57th Anti-Tank Regiment to any enthusiast of the 1940 France and Flanders Campaign; he sent me a copy which I have found to be very useful in filling gaps in my knowledge. Andy Newson has been an enormous help in supplying me with some of the relevant war diaries and accounts buried away in regimental histories; to him, and the members of the WW2 Talk Forum, I am extremely grateful. Jim Tuckwell has very kindly allowed me to use several pictures of the Durham Light Infantry at St-Venant from his excellent DLI website, which can be found at http://durhamlightinfantry.webs.com and assisted me with getting to grips with the St-Venant engagement. Peter Page sent me details of the French tank battles at St-Hilaire-Cottes and, in so doing, immediately improved my French language skills! I must also recognize the assistance given by the Public Records Office at Kew, the Imperial War Museum and the Army Museum.

On the ground I have been accompanied by David Rowland, Paul Webster and Tom Waterer. Their company has made each visit thoroughly enjoyable and has contributed much to the suggested routes and car tours found in Chapter 9. Lastly, but by no means least, my wife Joan has tolerated my absence across the water with her usual understanding and tolerance. Apart from those photographs that I have privately sourced, the remainder have largely come from my own personal collection. The Walk 2 and 3 maps have been drawn by Rebecca Jones of Glory Designs in Coventry. All mistakes in the text are entirely mine and while I have made every effort to trace copyright holders of the material used, I crave the indulgence of literary executors or copyright holders where these efforts have so far failed and would encourage them to contact me through the publisher so that any error can be rectified.

Jerry Murland
Coventry 2018

Chapter One

The Strategic Situation

The German offensive into France and Flanders began on 10 May 1940 with Army Group B, under *Generaloberst* Fedor von Bock, attacking through north-eastern Belgium and the main thrust of the German panzer divisions – Army Group A – under *Generaloberst* Gerd von Rundstedt advancing through the Ardennes to turn north and cut through the British and French lines. To the south, Army Group C, under the command of *Generaloberst* Ritter von Leeb, were tasked with neutralizing the Maginot Line fortifications. Dubbed 'the Matador's Cloak' by Basil Liddell Hart, the German plan adopted the code word *Fall Gelb*.

The British Expeditionary Force
In command of the BEF was 53-year-old General Lord Gort, a former Grenadier Guards officer who had served in the First World War with some distinction. Wounded on four occasions, he had been decorated with the Military Cross (MC) and the Distinguished Service Order (DSO) and two bars. His award of the coveted Victoria Cross (VC) came whilst he was commanding the 1ˢᵗ Battalion during the battle on the Canal du Nord in 1918. By 1935 he had been promoted to Major General and three years later, after a short tenure as Military Secretary to the Secretary of State for War, Leslie Hore-Belisha, he was appointed Chief of the Imperial General Staff (CIGS). There is no doubt that his appointment as CIGS had a great deal to do with his war record and Hore-Belisha's misplaced desire for the army to be led by a man of proven courage on the battlefield.

Lord Gort in conversation with Air Vice Marshal Charles Blount, AOC of the British Air Component in France.

If Gort's appointment as CIGS was met with a degree of bewilderment, then his subsequent confirmation on 1 September 1939 as Commander-in-Chief of the BEF drew gasps of disbelief, particularly from General Sir Edmund Ironside, who had been confidently expecting command of the BEF and now found himself appointed CIGS in Gort's place. But despite the barrage of criticism that faced his appointment, it has to be said, whatever his faults may have been, when the situation facing the BEF became desperate in the last days of May, Gort maintained his composure and grasp of the situation.

Plan D

Allied forces were under the overall command of Général Maurice Gamelin, a small, plump individual whose vision for the defence of France lay very much bound up with the construction of the static Maginot Line, which began in earnest in 1930 along the Franco-German border. Therein lay the Achilles heel of French fortune, as political and financial considerations determined it was 'incomplete' in 1939 and the chain of mutually supportive fortifications petered out north of Montmédy. Consequently, when the BEF arrived in France one of their principle tasks – along with the French – was to extend the Maginot Line defences along the border with Belgium to the North Sea. British General Headquarters (GHQ) was opened at Habarcq and Arras, and it was from there that the progress of the British military build-up in France was directed.

The chain of command in France and Flanders was unwieldy to say the least. The BEF technically came under the jurisdiction of Général Georges' North-East Front command, whose HQ was at La Ferté-sous-Jouarre, some forty miles east of Paris. From January 1940 Georges reported directly to Gamelin at his Vincennes HQ in the eastern suburbs of Paris. Once the BEF had taken up its positions along the Franco-Belgian frontier it became a small part of 65-year-old Général Gaston

Général Alphonse
Georges with Lord
Gort in Arras in
May 1940.

Billotte's Army Group, which was responsible for the front line from the North Sea to the beginning of the Maginot line. Included in his command was the French Seventh Army (Henri Giraud), the First Army (Georges Blanchard), the Ninth Army (André Corap) and the Second Army (Charles Huntziger). The confusion of command was to a great extent exacerbated by the lack of communication; written messages were either carried by dispatch rider or communicated via the telephone system and Gamelins' HQ had no radio communication at all! In the final days of the campaign Paris had to resort to using a link through London to communicate with Dunkerque. A similar state of affairs existed within the Air Forces, which were not under army control and were commanded by Général Joseph Vuillemin, who was answerable to the French Minister of Defence. Henri Giraud is on record as complaining that if even if he needed British aircraft to make a reconnaissance the procedure involved was elaborate:

Général Joseph Vuillemin commanded the French Air Force.

I have to ask Général Georges who asks Général Gamelin, who asks Marshal Barratt, who asks Vice Marshal Blount, who has a reconnaissance made for me, but more often than not long after it would have been of any real use. [Barratt and Blount commanded the British air forces in France]

It was on this shaky chain of command that the success of the France and Flanders campaign depended.

Gamelin's first proposal for countering the threat of invasion focussed on the less risky Plan E, which called for Allied forces to advance to the line of the Escaut. Despite this plan being the more sensible, it was discarded in favour of the more easterly River Dyle; Gamelin successfully arguing that the anti-tank defences built by the Belgians would allow for a rapid deployment and allow the French Seventh Army to link-up with the Dutch via Breda.

Thus, the strategic plan – which became known as Plan D – was for French and British forces to cross the border in the event of a German attack and occupy the line of the River Dyle, which runs roughly north and south about thirty miles east of Brussels. The BEF were to deploy between Louvain and Wavre, with the French First Army under Général Georges Blanchard on the right in the Gembloux Gap and the Belgians who, it was anticipated, would fall back into the gap between the left of the BEF and the right of the Général Henri Giraud's Seventh Army.

The Dyle Line

The 10 May signalled the end of the so-called Phoney War and the move east to the River Dyle. The main fighting force was headed by motorcycle units of 4/Royal Northumberland Fusiliers and 12th Lancers and was carried out, with little interference from enemy activity, by the troop carrying companies of the Royal Army Service Corps (RASC). Gort's plan was to place the 1st and 2nd Divisions on the right flank and the 3rd Division on the left, astride Louvain. By way of reserve the 48th (South Midland) Division was ordered to move east of Brussels and the 4th and 50th (Northumbrian) Divisions to the south. In addition, the 44th (Home Counties) Division was under orders to march to the Escaut south of Oudenaarde and the 42nd (East Lancashire) Division placed on readiness to take up station to their right if needed.

The Phoney War was the term applied to the period of military inactivity that existed in France and Flanders until the German invasion on May 10.

Events on the Meuse

Unbeknown at the time to British commanders was the extent of the German thrust by Army Group A, which had had struck the French Second Army on the Meuse. German advances late on the 13th had hastened a disorganized French retreat, which twenty-four hours later had become a rout, opening up a dangerous gap. Blanchard had little choice but to order a retirement to avoid being outflanked, which in its turn involved the British I Corps swinging their line back to the River Lasane to conform to the French retirement. For the I Corps units dug in along the Dyle, their initial surprise at being ordered to retire was replaced by the realization that the manoeuvre was to be carried out immediately and under the cover of darkness.

Although the Lasne was a poor substitute for the larger Dyle – which in itself was little more than a ditch in places – the BEF was intact and still full of fighting spirit. However, their movements now were dictated by a wider strategic picture, which had begun to threaten the whole Allied campaign. On the 16 May Gort issued his orders for a general withdrawal to the line of the River Senne, having first sent Major General Thomas Eastwood to Caudry to learn of Gaston Billotte's intentions. Billotte had reportedly burst into tears when informed of the German breakthrough along the Meuse. Some historians have argued that the lightening German panzer advance across France was reason enough for his tears; by 16 May armoured columns from Army Group A had advanced so rapidly into French territory that momentarily they lost contact with their headquarters because they had gone beyond field radio range.

The Escaut
But there was to be no rest along the line of the Senne, which for the retreating British units was only a temporary respite before fresh orders sent them back towards the line of the Escaut. What was hoped, by some, to be the point where the German advance was halted, only developed into another battle where the overwhelming might of Army Group B proved to be too much for the defending Allied forces. Gort, to his eternal credit, was apparently not convinced and had already moved any available units onto the Canal Line in preparation for the eventual evacuation from the Channel Ports. The fighting along the Escaut is described in the Battleground Europe title, *Battle for the Escaut 1940*.

As we know, events further south had already undermined any plan to stand on the Escaut and the visit by Billotte to Gort's HQ on the evening of 18 May finally furnished the British Commander-in-Chief with the detail of the panzer breakthrough in the south. By this juncture in the campaign the French command structure was beginning to crumble into disarray and, in an air of desperation, the 73-year-old Général Maxime Weygand was drafted in from North Africa to replace Gamelin as the Supreme Allied Commander. But the battle was already lost and no one

Général Maxime Weygand replaced Général Maurice Gamelin on 18 May as the Supreme Allied Commander.

summed up the disaster that had befallen France better than Weygand, who is reported to have said,' we have gone to war with a 1918 army against a German Army of 1939. It is sheer madness.'

The Arras Counterstroke

While Allied forces were fighting along the Escaut, the situation in the south grew even more threatening, with the German armoured spearhead reaching the channel coast on 20 May. This audacious drive for the coast effectively isolated Allied forces south of the Somme River from those in the north. The Arras counterstroke on 21 May was much too weak to be a serious threat but it did delay the German advance and inflicted significant losses on *Generalmajor* Erwin Rommel's 7th Panzer Division. Certainly Rommel's exaggerated claims of being attacked by five divisions at Arras did much to fuel the expectation of an Allied counter attack within the ranks of OKH (German Supreme High Command) and contributed to two halt orders and ultimately, the escape of the BEF from Dunkerque. Arras was evacuated by British troops on the night of 23 May.

The Halt Order of 21 May

It is highly likely that without this twenty-four hour intervention, the famous Hitler Halt Order of 24 May, would not have had the effect it did, as Dunkerque would have already been in German hands. It is a sad fact the Allies were too weak and disorganized to take advantage of the bruised momentum of Rommel's division at Arras; had they been able to make a combined attack from both north and south of the Somme, the panzers may well have been cut off from their supply lines and become isolated along the Channel coast. Whilst it was clear to most Allied observers that the counter attack was not going to take place, the *threat* of such an attack led to the order to halt the advance of the panzer divisions on 21 May. However, at this critical juncture in the Dunkerque story, the threat to the panzer divisions

Generalmajor **Erwin Rommel commanded the 7th Panzer Division in May 1940.**

no longer came from a counter attack but from the simple fact that the BEF *might* reach the Channel Ports before the Germans. It was a notion that had already crossed the mind of the British, who responded with a transfer of troops from the British mainland to Boulogne and Calais in order to block the German advance towards Dunkerque. The race for the Channel Ports was on.

Boulogne and Calais

It was not until the evening of 21 May that *General de Panzertruppen* Heinz Guderian and his XIX Panzer Corps was ordered to move north and capture the Channel Ports. His immediate plan was for the 10th Panzer Division to move on Dunkerque, the 2nd Panzer Division to seize Boulogne and the 1st Panzer Division to advance on Calais. Then, perhaps with the taste of the Arras Counterstroke still in mind, von Rundstedt held back the 10th Panzer Division, withdrawing them from Guderian's command and placing them in reserve. Although the 10th Panzer Division was restored to Guderian's command on 22 May and redirected to Calais, the damage had already been done and the opportunity of seizing the Channel Ports had evaporated. It took the 2nd Panzer Division three days to capture Boulogne, with the infantry finally overwhelming the garrison on 25 May; and even longer to take Calais, which was captured on 26 May. The account of the fighting in these two ports is looked at in detail in Jon Cooksey's *Boulogne – 20 Guard's Brigade Fighting Defence* and *Calais – A Fight to the Finish*.

General de Panzertruppen **Heinz Guderian.**

The Halt Order of 24 May

Known more generally as the Hitler Halt Order, which was sent to all German units west of the Canal Line, it remains one of the most hotly argued issues of the Second World War. On 24 May German forces were within ten miles of Dunkerque, which was the only remaining port north of the Somme River open to the evacuation of the BEF. The leading elements had already crossed the Aa Canal and there were no British or French troops capable of stopping the German Panzers from denying the port to the British and trapping about one million Allied troops in a rapidly reducing pocket of resistance. Hitler was on the threshold of a monumental victory yet, astonishingly, German OKH issued the order to halt the advance at 12.45 on 24 May. Loitering behind the order was the rising crescendo of disagreements between OKH and the officer corps, which escalated on 23 May, culminating in the removal of the Fourth Army from Army Group A and transferring it to Army Group B. In simple terms this meant that from 8.00pm on 24 May all panzer divisions would take their orders from von Bock and von Rundstedt would be concerned only with a flank protection along the Somme.

Generaloberst Gerd von Rundstedt (third from left) in conversation with Georg von Sodenstern, Julius von Bernuth and August Winter at the funeral of Erwin Rommel. August Winter can be seen standing behind von Rundstedt.

Hitler was furious and immediately rescinded the order, his anger focussing not only on the fact it had been made without his approval, but because he, too, had feelings of anxiety regarding the exposed nature of the panzer thrust and shared von Rundstedt's desire for the infantry to close the gap between the panzers. Thus the order issued by von Rundstedt's HQ was as follows:

> *On orders of the Führer, the attack to the east of Arras is to be continued with VIII Corps and, to the northwest, II Corps in cooperation with the left wing of Army Group B. The general line Lens-Béthune-Aire – St. Omer-Gravelines will not be crossed northwest of Arras.*

Hitler gave von Rundstedt complete freedom with regard to the length of the stop, a decision which was recorded by Alfred Jodl, Chief of the Wehrmacht Operations Staff, in his diary on 25 May. But, perhaps more to the point, was von Rundstedt's view that Army Group A would be needed for the eventual swing south of the Somme to force the capitulation of the trapped French Army; and that the remnants of the BEF could in fact be finished off by *Generaloberst* Fedor von Bock's

Army Group B and the *Luftwaffe*. It was not until the afternoon of 26 May that Hitler gave permission for the advance on Dunkerque to be continued. Whatever the reasons behind the Halt Order it was a very costly mistake and, even though he tried later to put all the blame on Hitler, the chief architect of the order was the wily von Rundstedt, upon whose head must lie much of the blame for ultimate failure of German forces to achieve the total destruction of the BEF.

The bulk of the German Army in 1940 was still largely horse drawn and the increasing gap between them and the panzers of Army Group A gave OKH some anxious moments.

The Canal Line
Gort's great fear of the Germans driving forward behind his right flank was becoming a reality and, with the BEF now fighting on two fronts, his response took the form of a number of *ad-hoc* battle groups, tasked with specific duties of defence. The line to be defended followed the canalized River Aa from Gravelines on the Channel coast, through St-Omer and La Bassée, to Raches, six miles north-east of Douai, and followed the old line of French fortified towns, which had already played a significant part in French military history. The Canal Line was the only natural barrier that stood any possibility of hindering the armoured advance of Army Group A from driving into the rear of the BEF.

Defending the Canal Line

The formation of improvised forces is a feature of Gort's conduct of the campaign and possibly had its origins in the German *Michael* offensive of March 1918, where Grover's Force on the Fifth Army front was one of the first of the 'scarecrow' armies put into the line in a desperate bid to stem the German advance. Gort's adoption of these hastily organised forces came under some criticism as many of the units involved were badly equipped, lacked battlefield experience and had little or no opportunity to make sound administrative arrangements. However, in reality there was little alternative; until the main British Expeditionary Force retired from the Escaut, the regularly organised and equipped infantry divisions were fully committed and none could be freed for the protection of the flank and rear. It was hoped that the defence these groups put up would be enough to deter von Rundstedt by making him hesitate before committing his armour. In the event it was not only the watery Canal Line which delayed the panzers but also the Halt Order of 24 May.

The first of these *ad-hoc* forces was Macforce, under Major General Noel Mason-Macfarlane. Created on 17 May, it was initially ordered to hold the line of the River Scarpe between Raches and St-Amand before it eventually moved north and was disbanded at Cassel on 25 May. Gort created three further formations under the names of Polforce , Usherforce and Rustyforce, each with specific orders to hold the line of the canals from Gravelines to Raches. His choice of which units to deploy relied very much on availability, hence the mix and match approach to defence that was evident at the main crossing points south of Gravelines.

German Dispositions on 23 May

Army Group A completed their dash to the Channel coast on 20 May when the 3rd Battalion of the 2nd Rifle Regiment finally dipped their feet in the sea near Noyelles. Panzer Gruppe Kleist was now intent on completing the advance by reducing Boulogne and Calais and denying Dunkerque to the BEF. Further south, Panzer Gruppe Hoth were heading north after their encounter with a mixed force from the 50th Division and 1 Army Tank Brigade at Arras on 21 May.

Paul Ewald von Kleist.

Panzer Group Kleist

Kleist's units were ranged along the Canal Line from Gravelines to Isbergues, with XIX Panzer Corps, under Heinz Guderian, in the north and XXXXI Panzer Corps,

10

under Georg-Hans Reinhardt, to the south. In addition to the two panzer corps, Kleist also had Gustav von Wietersheim's XIV Motorized Corps under his command. Following the conclusion of the war in 1945 (he was 59 years old in 1940), Ewald von Kleist died in the Vladimir Central Prison in 1954 after being extradited to the Soviet Union.

XIX Panzer Corps

On 23 May the 2nd Panzer Division (Rudolf Veiel) were attacking Boulogne and the 10th Panzer Division (Ferdinand Schaal) were at Calais, which did not fall until 26 May. The 1st Panzer Division (Friedrich Kirchner), together with Infantry Regiment *Grossdeutchland* and the SS-Division *Leibstandarte* Adolf Hitler (LSSAH), which had only recently come under Guderian's command, were ordered to the Aa Canal to secure the bridgeheads. *Grossdeutchland* was commanded by *Oberstleutnant* Wilhelm-Hunert von Stockhausen and, contrary to a number of publications, was a regular Wehrmacht regiment and not part of the Waffen-SS. The LSSAH was commanded by *Obergruppenfüher* Joseph Sepp Dietricht, who was sentenced to life imprisonment after the war for his part in the Malmedy massacre. Released on parole in 1955 he was arrested again a year later

Obergruppenfüher **Joseph Sepp Dietrich commanded the** *SS-Leibstandarte* **Adolf Hitler Division (LSSAH).**

for his role in the execution of the *Sturmbteilung* (SA) leaders during the so-called Night of the Long Knives in 1934. He was finally released in 1958 and died eight years later. Guderian and his staff surrendered to US forces in May 1945 and he remained a prisoner until his release in June 1948. He died in 1954.

XXXXI Panzer Corps

Georg-Hans Reinhardt's Corps included the 6th and 8th Panzer Divisions and the SS-*Verfügungs* Motorized Infantry. The 6th Panzer Division was under the command of Werner Kempf, while Adolph-Friedrich Kuntzen commanded the 8th Panzer Division. The SS-*Verfügungs* Division was commanded by 60-year-old Paul Hausser. The

Georg-Hans Reinhardt was in command of XXXXI Panzer Corps.

division included three motorized infantry battalions, *Der Fuhrer*, *Deutschland* and *Germania*. Hausser was relieved of his command of Army Group Centre in April 1945 and ended the war on Albert Kesselring's staff. He died in 1972. Werner Kempf was released from Allied captivity in 1947 and the 51-year-old Adolph-Friedrich Kuntzen retired from active service in 1944. He died twenty years later, in 1964. Reinhardt was found guilty of war crimes in 1946 and sentenced to fifteen years imprisonment but was released in 1952. He died in 1963.

Panzer Gruppe Hoth

Herman Hoth's units were deployed along the Canal Line from Isbergues to Carvin, XVI Panzer Corps were to the north and XXXIV Panzer Corps to the south, along with the 20th (Motorized) Division under the command of Mauritz von Wiltorin. It was the 20th Division that assaulted the 2/5 Leicesters at Pont-à-Vendin. The 55-year-old Hoth was another high ranking German officer convicted of war crimes in 1945; his sentence of fifteen years in prison ended in 1954 when he was released on parole.

Herman Hoth (right) in conversation with Heinz Guderian.

XVI Panzer Corps

In command was 54-year-old Eric Hoepner, a man who was later tortured and hanged in 1944 for his part in the Hitler assassination plot. Hoepner's command included the 3rd Panzer Division (Horst Stumpff), the 4th Panzer Division (Ludwig Ritter von Radlmeier) and the SS-*Totenkopf* Division (Theodor Eicke), which had been badly mauled at Arras during the Allied counterstroke. It was Eicke's division that was responsible for the massacre of the Royal Norfolk's at Louis Creton's farm on 27 May. The 48-year-old Eicke was killed in February 1943 during the Third Battle of Kharkov and von Radlmeier retired from active service in 1941.

Theodore Eicke commanded the SS-*Totenkopf* Division.

XXXIV Panzer Corps

Rudolf Schmidt was 54-years-old when he was appointed to command XXXIV Corps in February 1940. His formation included the 5th Panzer Division (Max von Hartlieb-Walsporn) and the redoubtable Erwin Rommel with his 7th Panzer Division, who had also been involved in the clash at Arras on 21 May. Rommel went on to have a glittering army career but he was implicated in the plot to assassinate Hitler in 1944 and he was given a choice between committing suicide, in return for assurances that his family would not be persecuted following his death, or a trial that would result in his execution. He chose suicide. Von Hartlieb-Walsporn was badly wounded in May 1942, which effectively ended any further active service; after the war he was captured and imprisoned for two years. Schmidt was arrested by Soviet forces in 1947 and imprisoned at the Vladimir Central and Butyrka prisons. In 1952, he was sentenced to twenty-five years but released in 1955. He died two years later.

Chapter Two

Usherforce

On 10 May 1940 Headquarters of the X Force Lines of Communication (X L of C) troops, under the command of Colonel Charles 'Dougie' Usher, was established at Avesnes with the object of administering the area vacated by the BEF as it moved forward into Belgium under the terms of Plan D. The 49-year-old Usher had been captured at Le Cateau in 1914 while fighting with 1/Gordon Highlanders and spent the remainder of the war behind the wire as a prisoner. In January 1938 he achieved one of his life's ambitions and took command of the battalion, taking it to France with the 51st (Highland) Division in September 1939. It was to be a short lived tenure, as in February 1940 he handed over to Lieutenant Colonel Harry Wright, and embarked on a new role as Area Commandant at St-Malo in Brittany, with the rank of colonel. Usher may have been classed amongst those elderly senior officers who were not up to the rigours of battlefield leadership, but his move to St-Malo did at least avoid another long term of captivity when the survivors of his old battalion were taken prisoner at St-Valery-en-Caux on 12 June. In April 1940 Usher was moved again, this time to take command of X L of C with Major Thomas 'Harry' Jefferies at his Deputy Assistant Quartermaster General (DAQMG). This was intended to be an appointment well in the rear of the fighting

Charles Usher took command of Usherforce on 23 May.

but, with the tide of war very much against the Allies, Usher was destined to be caught up in the fighting as the BEF withdrew towards Dunkerque.

It would have been apparent to Gort by 15 May that a German threat was developing against the right flank and rear of the BEF, which accounts for Usher's collection of artillery, machine guns and infantry, swinging northwards to enable communication with the BEF to be based on Dunkerque, Calais and Boulogne. Days later Usher moved his headquarters to Béthune and then, on 22 May, to Socx, which was organized into a defence locality. Here, information was received that enemy forces were to the west of the River Aa between Gravelines and St-Omer.

Usherforce was formed on 23 May and placed under Charles Usher's command. His orders were to take command of all troops in the area, including the remnants of the 23rd Division, and move his headquarters to Bergues, where the garrison was said to 'be out of control' and hold the line of the River Aa from Gravelines to St-Omer, a distance of some twenty miles. But, as the French moved west to stem the German advance towards Dunkerque, Usherforce withdrew its units from the northern end of the canal to focus on defending Bergues and the approaches to Dunkerque, leaving Polforce to defend the line of the canal further south. However, the area allocated to each of the two forces tended to overlap and at the St-Momelin and St-Omer bridges some units, ostensibly under orders from both Usherforce and Polforce, found themselves defending the same sector.

By 21 May the German forces had trapped the BEF in an area along the northern coast of France. Evacuation via Dunkerque was becoming the only option.

Usher's force consisted of one inexperienced and under-equipped infantry battalion from 69 Brigade, three units of artillery and a collection of searchlight troops from 5/Searchlight Brigade. In addition, he had at his disposal the troops from the 23rd Division Reception Camp at Bollezeele and a handful of engineers from 233/Field Squadron. His command, for the most part, consisted of the following units:

6/Green Howards
3/(Ulster) Searchlight Regiment
1/Super Heavy Battery at St-Pierre Brouck
3/Super Heavy Battery at Watten
52/Super Heavy Regiment at St-Momelin
Lieutenant Colonel Oliver Cobbett's 23rd Divisional Force

The Gravelines garrison was under the command of Major Cordier, who commanded the 6th Battalion, 310th Regiment of Infantry, an individual whom the Green Howard's regimental historian portrayed as an 'elderly colonel' who considered himself to be the garrison commander. Synge writes that:

[Cordier] *was only persuaded with great difficulty that the Green Howards were correct in taking up their positions facing south-west, while his own troops, except for some mortars covering the estuary, were facing east.*

This looks to be an unfair criticism. While Cordier may indeed have been elderly it is highly unlikely that he and the Gravelines garrison were unaware of what was taking place along the coast at Boulogne and Calais, particularly as some elements of Général Pierre Lanquetot's 21st Division had already fallen back on Gravelines after the fighting in and around Boulogne. Despite being described as 'out of touch with the situation', a number of French units were already at Gravelines and further south along the canal towards Watten and were very clearly *in touch* with the strategic situation.

3/(Ulster) Searchlight Regiment

The regiment was commanded by Lieutenant Colonel Frederick Wallace, a decorated veteran of the First World War, and consisted of four searchlight batteries, each made up of four troops. Formed only three days before war was declared, apart from one troop of 10 Battery, which were at Arras, the regiment's batteries were deployed relatively close together in and around the Dunkerque area and were some of the first British troops to reach the canal at Gravelines.

Officer and men of the searchlight regiments were drafted in to garrison the main crossing points at Gravelines and points south.

Wallace realized that it was imperative to delay the enemy long enough to allow French troops to get into position and prevent German armoured divisions from reaching Dunkerque.

E Troop, 10 Battery

Lieutenant Allen and his troop were ordered to Gravelines on 21 May to assist the French in barricading the three bridges over the canal and the bridge on D229 at Les Targette. Each bridge was clearly identified in Lieutenant Allen's notes :

It was found that four bridges in all had to be dealt with:
The main bridge on the Calais-Dunkerque road (Bridge 1)
A smaller bridge connected with the same road via a quayside road (Bridge 2)
A railway bridge (Bridge 3)some 500 yards south of Bridge 2
The bridge at Les Targette (Bridge 4)
Bridges 1 and 4 were swing bridges and could be swung open whenever desirable; Bridge 3 was also a swing bridge but could not be opened until absolutely necessary on account of the railway traffic.

J Troop, 11 Battery

The troop moved from Cassel to Gravelines under the command of Lieutenant Dunn on 21 May and took over the defence of the left flank Gravelines bridges – Bridges 2 and 3 – on 22 May.

K Troop, 11 Battery

The troop arrived at les Huttes with Second Lieutenant Armstrong in command at 3.30am on 22 May and was ordered to take command of all three bridges at Gravelines. Concerned at the potential lack of communication between K Troop and Dunn's J Troop, Armstrong focussed his attention on the main swing bridge on the Calais road – Bridge 1, leaving the remaining two bridges to J Troop. Positioning eight machine gun posts to cover the approaches to the bridge, along with two anti-tank rifles, he also writes of French 75mm guns operating from the walls of the Arsenal behind him:

At 9.00am on 24 May an enemy tank appeared on the bridge and was immediately put out of action by a French 75mm gun firing from the bastion. My forward Lewis gunners opened fire on what they took to be enemy machine guns. Very soon the enemy was shelling us with what appeared to be guns similar to the French 75mm and concentrated on two of our Lewis guns. After one gun had been badly damaged, Lance Sergeant Hurst took both guns out of their pits and installed them in alternative positions.

At 3.00pm, with the enemy having made no headway across the bridge, Armstrong was ordered to hand over control of his defences to the French and withdraw to Leffrinckoucke.

L Troop, 11 Battery

Lieutenant Boycott's troop took up positions at Les Targette swing bridge at 3.30pm on 22 May, where he was joined by two French 75mm guns and their crews from 402 Régiment d'Artillerie. At 6.30pm, after machine gun fire was heard from the direction of St-Folquin. Boycott ordered the bridge to be swung open and the blocking vehicles moved into position. Soon after this, advanced scouts from 1st Panzer Division in the form of two German motorcycle combinations approached and were fired upon by the French 75mm guns. A short lull was followed by the appearance of a tank, which was instantly disabled by the French guns. Boycott, who was the only junior officer in the regiment to have received any sort of ground defence training, took immediate steps to prevent his position from being outflanked:

> *The enemy then spread out in the neighbouring fields and opened machine gun fire. The bridge defenders were also fired on by guns from the enemy AFVs and the shells appeared to be of the 3-pounder size. At about 8.15pm I saw various parties of the enemy spreading out to our right and led a party, consisting of Bombardier Blair and Lance Bombardier Patterson with a Lewis gun, to a high bank about 500yards to the north to prevent any enemy enfilade fire.*

Having opened fire on any available target, Boycott left Blair and Patterson with the Lewis gun to hold the position until relieved – which they were at 3.30am on 24 May – and returned to the bridge where, fortunately, the enemy fire had slackened with the approaching darkness. At 10.30am Bombardier William Gilbert, with two cans of petrol, crossed the canal by boat and attempted to destroy the bridge. It would appear that this was not completely successful as he tried again the following day. With the onset of darkness L Troop were reinforced by forty men from E Troop, 10/Battery, and Boycott writes that they managed to snatch a few hours sleep. At 5.20am on 24 May the German assault began again:

> *Machine gun fire again opened up by the enemy. The men of my troop took up their positions on the river bank. At 5.35am the enemy started shelling with field guns of a similar calibre to the British 18-pounders. This was combined with strong and continuous machine gun fire. The French guns returned fire until*

18

The speed of the advance of the German Panzer divisions took the Allies by surprise.

their ammunition was expended and then the gun crews left at about 6.30am.

Despite French shelling continuing from Bourbourg, which Boycott says had no effect on the German guns at all, the weight of fire from the western side of the canal was too much for the beleaguered men of 3/Searchlight Regiment and by 1.00pm the position was evacuated by Second Lieutenant Trist after the officer commanding a Green Howard detachment at the St-Nicolas bridge had sent word he had been ordered to withdraw. Casualties were remarkably light, with only seven men wounded in L Troop; but E Troop were shelled while moving up to Les Targette in the early hours of 24 May, losing two men killed and three wounded. Allen and Boycott were mentioned in despatches and Bombardier Gilbert received the MM.

6/Green Howards, 69 Brigade, 23rd Division
The battalion was brought up to strength at the beginning of September 1939 under the command of Lieutenant Colonel Matthew 'Rex' Steel DSO, MC. On 20 May they were in position, east of Arras, along the north bank of the River Scarpe at Roeux, with the 5/East Yorkshires at Plouvain under Lieutenant Colonel Daniel Keating. As a largely untrained and badly equipped battalion of men, who had been previously employed as a 'pick and shovel battalion', the fact that the Germans made no attempt to cross the river must have resulted in profound relief all round. In the early hours of 21 May the battalion was replaced in the line by

4/Green Howards from the 50th Division and given orders to retire to Farbus. As recounted in the Battleground Europe title, *Frankforce and the Defence of Arras 1940*, the bulk of 70 Brigade had been overrun on 20 May and reduced to little more than a handful of men by the powerful 8th Panzer Division. This had in effect reduced the 60-year-old Major General William Herbert's 23rd Division to not much more than a single brigade of infantry.

Steel took over temporary command of 69 Brigade on 22 May, devolving command of the battalion to Major George Dixon. Later that day orders were received for the 23rd Division to withdraw north and deploy along the right bank of the River Aa at Gravelines. However, reports of German panzers in or near Hazebrouck and enemy air activity along the road leading north, resulted in the convoy being turned back at Estaires after a frantic search by divisional staff officers. In the event, only 6/Green Howards made it to Gravelines, along with Advanced Divisional Headquarters. Just after dawn on 23 May the battalion, now reunited with Lieutenant Colonel Steel, took up positions along the canalized River Aa.

The Green Howards' war diary tell us that Steel deployed his battalion along the canal 'from the sea to the junction of the river and canal' for some seven miles from Petit Fort Phillipe to the small bridge at St-Nicolas, which is mentioned by Lieutenant Boycott in his account of K Troop's battle at Les Targette. It should be said that there is still a bewildering confusion to be found in a number of sources regarding the date of the Green Howards' arrival at Gravelines and the subsequent action that involved Second Lieutenant John Hewson and 13 Platoon. For the sake of consistency, the author is using dates and times referred to in the war diary, which appears to be largely correct.

3/Royal Tank Regiment (3/RTR)
The officers and men of 3/RTR were landed at Calais on 22 May with the task of 'mopping up some isolated pockets of German tanks which were operating in the area between Boulogne and Calais.' On 23 May orders to proceed directly to St-Omer were received with instructions to protect GHQ at Hazebrouck, but having run into the 1st Panzer Division at Guines and being ordered back into Calais, Major Bill Reeves and his four tanks were the only armoured vehicles from his regiment to get out of Calais before the garrison surrendered. According to Reeves' account, he arrived at the swing bridge at Gravelines on the Calais road at about 2.00am on 24 May with three light tanks from Lieutenant Peter William's troop and his own A13 Cruiser tank armed with a 2-pounder gun. Reeves says he got in touch with the captain in command of some of the Provost

An A13 Cruiser Mark III of the type used by Major Bill Reeves. The picture shows one of the 3/RTR tanks abandoned at Calais.

Corps, [who would have arrived with the 23rd Division Advanced Headquarters] who gave him some idea of the situation:

At about 5.00am on Friday 24th, I gleaned more information and got in touch with the local French commander at Gravelines and offered to assist him in the defence of the town, which he assured me was in for a terrific bombardment and attack that very day. I went round the defences with him and strongly advised him to blow the bridges over the canal which ran round the western half of the town. This he would not do, partly because the French never will blow their bridges and partly because of the short space of time for the preparation.

Capitaine Clement Morel, who was acting as Cordier's chief of staff, recalls meeting Reeves close to the western bastion:

The major commanding this squadron explains to me that he comes from Calais, and that, surprising as it is, he has during the night advanced on the road between a large number of German tanks and vehicles, the soldiers resting on the grass both sides of the road ... Major Cordier, being desirous to include this

21

unexpected valuable force in his defence system. I asked this British major if he was willing to stay with us a few more hours before proceeding to Dunkerque.

Reeves was only too happy to accept and took up position between Bridges 1 and 2 to await the arrival of the 1st Panzer Division.

24 May 1940

The forward reconnaissance units of the 1st Panzer Division appeared around 9.00am, when a few light tanks approached the bridge on the Calais road and were fired on. Present at the bridge was 13 Platoon, Green Howards, which was under the command of 20-year-old Lieutenant John Hewson. The platoon had been entrusted with the company's single Boys anti-tank rifle, which Hewson decided to handle himself. Positioning himself and the anti-tank rifle well forward of his platoon, he knocked out the first tank and hit several others. Major Leslie Petch, commanding B Company, recalled refugees trying to rush the bridge, followed by three enemy tanks:

Major Leslie Petch commanded B Company, 6/Green Howards.

We fired on the tanks and fortunately stopped the rushing of the bridge. It was here that John Hewson, firing an anti-tank rifle, was hit by a mortar and killed. It was reported he stopped two tanks [sic] with his [anti-tank] rifle.

Whether or not Hewson actually hit the German tank or not is unimportant, as there appeared to be a considerable weight of effective fire directed by the defending force – albeit a little uncoordinated. What is strange is that no mention is made by the Green Howards of Lieutenant Armstrong and K Troop or indeed Lieutenant Dunn's J Troop, who were defending Bridges 2 and 3. Armstrong's troop was also manning the bridge defences on the Calais road and was evidently in the thick of the fighting and must have liaised with Hewson over fields of fire and deployment. Quite who was responsible for knocking out the enemy tanks at the Calais road bridge is thus unclear, but it would appear that Major Reeves and his tanks accounted for several of the enemy armoured vehicles:

The Battle of Gravelines did not take long to develop in earnest. The town was first bombarded with mortars and very soon afterwards I saw from the turret of my tank some refugees holding up their hands on the other side of the bridge. This was a sure signal that the Germans were close at hand and sure enough a few seconds later an armoured carrier and two tanks came over the crest just the other side of the bridge. Our chance had come therefore, they even said the 2-pounder gun had scored a hit on the armoured carrier.

The Green Howards' war diary tells us Reeves was on the western side of the canal, while Reeves himself says he was between the canal and the walls of the Bastion on the eastern side of the canal. It was after withdrawing from his position on the eastern bank of the canal back into the town that the A13 Cruiser was hit by what Reeves describes as a 'British anti-tank gunner' who mistook them for German tanks and 'let fly'. Here the accounts differ again, Reeves says one round penetrated his tank and severely wounded two of the crew, while the Green Howards regimental historian claims one crew member was killed and replaced by the Headquarters Company cook. Whatever the truth, it would appear that Reeves' tanks accounted for four more enemy vehicles before withdrawing to Bergues, leaving behind one light tank with a broken track. After a number of further adventures in and around Ypres, they were all evacuated from Dunkerque.

Meanwhile, 6/Green Howards, together with the assortment of British and French units, continued to deny the Gravelines crossings to the 1st Panzer Division. The 25mm anti-tank guns of the 18th Groupe de Reconnaissance de Corps d'Armée (GRCA) accounting for another seven German tanks before the fighting quietened down in the late afternoon. With Steel summoned to Bergues by Charles Usher, Major Dixon received orders at 6.00pm to withdraw the battalion to Fort Mardyck. The Green Howards move from Gravelines seems to have been somewhat premature, as Général Bertrand Fagalde, commanding the French XVI Corps, was still in the process of bringing in Général Beaufrère's 68th Infantry Division to take over the line of the Aa. The withdrawal of the Green Howards illustrated the confusion of responsibility that existed between the British and French forces in the area. Even to the most casual observer there appeared to be very little distribution of responsibility between the two Allied forces; both British and French detachments could be found holding the same positions at the same time but under two separate commands. This was a situation that exposed the weakness of the defenses along the Aa.

The Green Howards withdrawal was carried out under fire, the Germans, having crossed the canal at Les Targette and St-Pierre Brouck, intercepted Steel's men, resulting in some 'very confused hand-to-hand fighting on the outskirts of the town'. It is likely that a number of the fourteen Green Howard casualties in the nearby Oye-Plage Communal Cemetery may well have been killed in this encounter. However, despite the withdrawal of the British and the German advance south of the town, the French garrison at Gravelines held on until 29 May, even though the French units, who were defending the western sector of the Dunkerque perimeter, began their withdrawal to the line of the Mardyck Canal on 27 May. Sadly, Lieutenant Colonel Steel died in service in 1941 and is buried in Great Ayton Cemetery, North Yorkshire.

Le Cochon Noir
It is astonishing that the surviving war diaries only give a passing mention of the plight of Belgian civilians at Cochon Noir, where some 200 civilians were slaughtered by ground fire and aerial attack, after being caught between the advancing 1st Panzer Division and the defending French and British. On 23 May, travelling largely in private motor vehicles, a column of several thousand Belgian refugees had been prevented from crossing the swing bridge on the Calais to Dunkerque road by the French military authorities. Oscar Lecerf, a newspaper correspondent working with *Nord Matin*, reported the scene along the Calais road prior to the bridge being closed:

> *The cars pass without interruption, coming from Belgium recalling the exodus of 1914. Alas! It is the exodus of 1940 with its sad procession. These were the first luxurious cars of the notables of Belgium, followed by those of the officers fleeing the invasion, helping to sow panic throughout their passage, then passenger cars, vans loaded with clothes, lingerie and objects of value, all covered with mattresses.*

With the bridge on the Calais road swung open, some of the refugees then headed north to Grand Fort Phillipe but others chose to remain on the ground known as Cochon Noir. There is a fleeting reference to the bridge and the plight of the refugees in a letter written in 1969 by Clement Morel; he recalls the bridge being opened and describes the approach of the German armoured units:

> *The swinging bridge is swung across thus isolating soldiers and numerous civilians waiting on the left bank; they are told the bridge will not be used again and ordered to clear out without delay in view of the impending battle ... On the road from Calais*

The scene at the swing bridge on the Calais road at Gravelines. An abandoned vehicle, most likely belonging to the stream of Belgian refugees attempting to enter Gravelines, sits on the quayside, with the bridge firmly closed to road traffic.

many German tanks, armoured cars and guns have advanced through the files of motor cars held up on the other side of the river and reached the left bank.

In Major Bill Reeves account there is a reference to the bridge on the Calais road being briefly opened to road traffic on 24 May as the battle for Gravelines was just beginning – presumably between 8.00 and 9.00pm. Reeves wondered if it was the result of a fifth columnist or a kind hearted Frenchman. Major Leslie Petch of the Green Howards also remarks in his diary that the bridge on the Calais road was rushed by refugees who were later seen holding up their hands in surrender. The bombing was probably the result of Clement Morel's insistence on air support, which arrived in the form of three Blenheims and attacked the German units on Cochon Noir. Eduard Timerman, a young Belgian refugee from Dendermonde, was 10-years-old on 24 May and remembers the air attack:

The bombing began. My mother took me in his arms and we took refuge in a house near the bridge. I heard a huge noise and the house was blown, I fainted. When I regained my senses, the English or French air force bombed the area. I took refuge in a ditch near the port with a young man who was to be 18 years. He was killed at the next bombing and I found myself alone again. I saw this road strewn with corpses.

Eduard lost both parents in the attack and although his father, Philemon, lies in the cemetery at les Huttes, his mother remains unidentified. Today, the only reminder of those terrible events of 24 May is the memorial that was unveiled in May 2013.

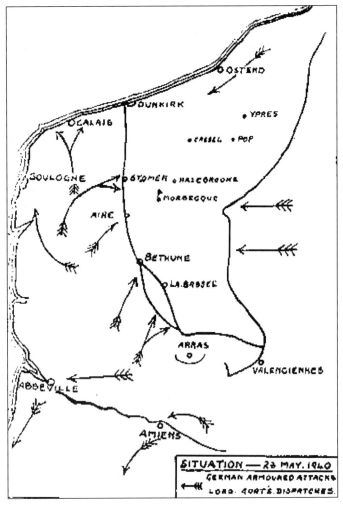

A sketch map drawn by Brigadier Gawthorpe illustrating the Canal Line from Gravelines to Valenciennes and the German advance up until 23 May.

1/Super Heavy Battery at St-Pierre Brouck

The Super Heavy batteries serving with the BEF in 1940 were equipped with two 9.2-inch or 12-inch guns of First World War vintage. The 1/Super Heavy Battery arrived in France on 25 March and was commanded by Major Henry Boxwell, a First World War veteran whose MC was gazetted in September 1918. The Battery moved from Fourquereuil Sandpits Sidings – south west of Béthune – on 20 May, arriving at St-Pierre Brouck at 3.00am on 23 May, where the battery was ordered to strengthen the French unit already guarding the swing bridge spanning the canal; it is unclear at this point whether the French had disabled the bridge or merely opened it. This French unit was probably an anti-aircraft detachment from 402 Régiment d'Artillerie and armed with a single 75mm self propelled anti-aircraft gun. German units from 1st Panzer Division were observed approaching the canal at 5.00am on 24 May and were greeted with rifle fire from the battery personnel. The war diary reports the French unit quickly withdrew 'abandoning the gun with four rounds', which the battery fired across the canal at enemy forces. By 11.00am the Germans had broken through and the battery withdrew.

The bridge at Holque

Attacked on 24 May by the 4th Panzer Reconnaissance Battalion from the 1st Panzer Division, this bridge was apparently not one which had been allocated to Usherforce and was defended by a battalion of the French 137th Regiment of Infantry. The French managed to halt the German advance until 7.30pm, after which they were forced back to a line running from Cappelle-Brouck to Pont l'Abbesse on the Haute-Colme Canal.

3/Super Heavy Battery at Watten

The battery should not be confused with 3/Super Heavy Regiment, which was disbanded in 1945. The unit arriving in France in March 1940 and was under the command of 42-year-old Major Percy Strudwick. Equipped with 12-inch Howitzers, it was under GHQ command. On 23 May Strudwick sent Second Lieutenant Cocks and ten men to the bridge at Watten with an anti-tank rifle, a party that Strudwick reinforced after hearing that enemy tanks were within three miles of the bridge; these may well have been the advanced units of the SS-*Liebstandarte* Adolf Hitler Division. Concerned that the Germans would break through, Usher sent one of his staff officers to Bollezeele with orders for Lieutenant

A 1933 recruiting poster for the SS-Division *Liebstandarte.*

27

Colonel Oliver Cobbett, commanding the 23rd Division Reception Camp, to take up a position astride the D226 with whatever personnel he could muster and prepare to hold the advancing panzers. Cobbett was a former member of the 4/Dragoon Guards, joining his regiment in France in 1917. Apart from being wounded at some point, little more is known of his career until he was given command of the reception camp at Bollezeele.

At 6.00pm Cocks reported that a French unit – most probably from the 27th Groupe de Reconnaissance – had entered Watten and taken up position on the main road and hill, east of the town. By 8.00pm three German armoured vehicles were in the station yard on the west bank of the canal, from where mortar fire was directed on the hill.

The railway station at Watten, from where the Germans opened up mortar fire on the heights above the town.

Just after midnight on 24 May, Cock's meagre garrison was reinforced by a party of around a hundred officers and men from 3/Army Field Workshops. Two hours later the first probing attack on the bridge commenced:

At 2.00am vehicles could be heard approaching the bridge. A searchlight from [one of the vehicles] swept over the canal. The vehicle stopped and men got out. At this stage the vehicles had not been identified as hostile. The vehicles then approached the barricade [on the bridge] and exposed a searchlight on the Lewis gun post and opened fire. We replied. The charge on the bridge was blown. A sharp exchange of fire took place for about five minutes. Our anti-tank guns were seriously handicapped by not having tracer ammunition or night firing attachments. The enemy AFVs were quickly turned round and raced back for cover. No casualties were suffered by our side

Strudwick writes that *Capitaine* Lemire and twenty men from the 59th Groupe de Reconnaissance, equipped with two anti-tank guns and machine guns, arrived at 3.00am from Bollezeele and was reinforced at 10.00am by two companies of the 14th Régiment Territorial de Travailleurs. Harrassed by sniper fire, Cocks and his party retired to the hill east of Watten, leaving the French garrison to man the bridge defences. At 4.30am, under orders from Strudwick, the British detachment informed the French of their departure and withdrew to les Moëres.

Grossdeutchland **was a regular Wehrmacht Regiment in XIX Panzer Corps. The photograph depicts a MG34 machine gun team.**

52/Heavy Regiment (Bedfordshire Yeomanry), Royal Artillery, at St-Momelin

In 1940 a heavy regiment consisted of four batteries, two of which were equipped with 7.2-inch howitzers and two with 155mm guns. The regiment arrived in France at the beginning of April 1940 under the command of 54-year-old Lieutenant Colonel Augustine Comerford, who was commissioned in 1916 into the Army Veterinary Service, transferring in 1931 to the Royal Artillery. Moving a heavy regiment and their guns

The men of 56/Heavy Regiment operating similar guns to that issued to the heavy batteries deployed along the canal.

to a new location was no easy matter in 1940 and even though the initial order to move was received at 11.00am on 21 May it was not until nearly six hours later that the Battery Reconnaissance Party arrived at St-Momelin in the afternoon, relieving the men of 8/Searchlight Battery. The three batteries of guns took considerably longer, not arriving at the bridge until 9.00am on 22 May, and were billeted in a deserted factory about one mile east of the village. By this time Regimental Head Quarters had been established in the château near the bridge and the commanding officer and his staff had no doubt benefitted from a relatively undisturbed night. At 9.00am on 22 May Brigadier John Gawthorpe, commanding 137 Brigade, arrived and gave instructions for the defence of the bridge, while a detachment of Royal Engineers prepared the bridge for demolition.

At Morbecque intelligence received by Gawthorpe suggested that German tanks were approaching St-Omer, which may have accounted for the rapid movement from Merville of X Company, 9/Royal Northumberland Fusiliers (9/RNF), under the command of 33-year-old Captain Ernest Hart, who had orders to guard the bridges between

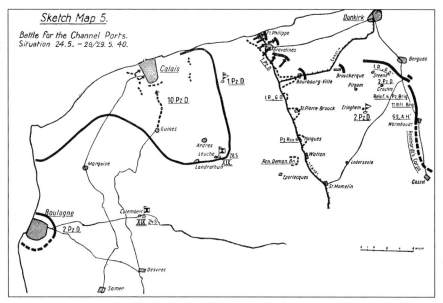

**A map from Heinz Guderian's *Panzer Leader* depicting the movements of
XIX Panzer Corps from 24 to 28 May 1940.**

Blaringhem and St-Momelin. It must have been a somewhat reassuring
sight for the men of 52/Heavy Regiment when the RNF convoy stopped
at the bridge in the late afternoon to leave Second Lieutenant Ross and
No 6 Platoon before continuing their journey south towards St-Omer.
Ross reported to Lieutenant Colonel Comerford at the château and was
deployed along the canal. The war diary also records the arrival of Second
Lieutenant George Peile and the E1 Section gun from 393/Battery,
98/Field Regiment and a platoon of Royal Welch Fusiliers from No 3
Company, Don Details. Gunner Les Cannon, a signaler serving with 52/
Heavy Regiment, remembered arriving in St-Momelin and being billeted
in the disused factory, which he describes as a former brickworks. The
next day he writes that 'we were posted to rifle, machine gun and anti
tank posts to defend the canal', and his post was in the roadway by the
side of a 25-pounder gun, which must have been the E1 Section gun. He
also noted a furious battle was taking place above him between
Hurricanes and Me109s.

At 3.00am on 23 May, Major Jeffreys received the following message
from Lieutenant Colonel Comerford at St-Momelin;

*I am at St-Momelin H1458 swing bridge which is swung open. I
have a telephone line with 1/Super Heavy Battery at Watten
H1263,2/Anti-Aircraft Brigade are at Rensecure and 2/Searchlight*

31

Regiment are about H2354 [Haute Schoubrouck]. *Am arranging W/T with them. 23 Division is at Bollezeele and the Chief Royal Engineers Officer* [Lieutenant Colonel John Kennedy] *is preparing all bridges for demolition from Gravelines to St-Omer... The colonel of French Territorials in St-Omer reports enemy strength at one battalion, with some motor cyclists and five or six tanks advancing on St-Omer from the south east and two larger columns moving westward having come from St-Pol.*

As dawn broke heavy artillery and machine gun fire from the opposite bank heralded the arrival of German forces, Charles Usher ordered the guns to be evacuated and for Comerford to leave a strong defending force at the bridge. His orders prompted a feverish improvement of the defensive positions and the demolition of the bridge at 5.00pm in anticipation of a strong German attack the next day. During the hours of darkness the enemy brought up a light mortar and established it behind the café on the opposite side of the canal, a move which failed to deter the defensive force from placing mines on the approaches to the bridge. At 7.00pm Comerford was summoned to Bergues and ordered to hand over the defence of the bridge to the French, who arrived some three hours later. Owing to the lateness of the hour, Comerford decided to withdraw during the hours of darkness on 25 May. The French, who were probably elements of the 21st Division of Infantry, clearly felt the British should stay and a heated discussion was followed by the French commander threatening to shoot any British soldiers that withdrew. Comerford was between a rock and a hard place, on one hand he had direct orders to retire and on the other he was faced with a belligerent Frenchman who threatened to open fire on any British who attempted to leave.

Meanwhile, on 25 May, the Germans brought up howitzers and proceeded to shell the village and bridge area, badly wounding 48-year-old Major Edward Williams and wounding Major Wall, who was on the higher ground south of the village. Both men were serving with 52/Heavy Regiment; sadly Williams later died of his wounds and is buried at Boulogne Eastern Cemetery. The French cookhouse in the château grounds was also hit, resulting in the death of two British and three French orderlies. Further heated discussion with the French continued and finally, at 1.00am, Comerford was able to rendezvous at the factory and commence his withdrawal to Crombeke. Gunner Cannon recalled none of this altercation but did remember the machine gun by the church was 'peppering away at enemy infantry on the other side of the canal'. Confirming Comerford's account, Cannon and his fellow signallers finally withdrew sometime after midnight, arriving in Crombeck early the next morning.

The bridges at St-Omer

Amongst the first troops from Usherforce to deploy at St-Omer was a battery from 2/Searchlight Regiment, who arrived in the town at 7.00pm on 21 May and barricaded the bridge by the railway station with searchlight vehicles. At 5.30am the next morning they were informed that Polforce were taking over the defence of the St-Omer bridges in the form of No 3 Company of the Don Details, under the command of Captain Wilfred Bickford of the Royal Berkshire Regiment. The Don Details battalion was formed on 19 May from officers and men at the leave transit camp at Don and was commanded by Major Barber, who organized his men into six companies, each company consisting of three platoons. Bickford writes that they were desperately short of equipment:

We had no Bren guns or anti-tank rifles, 50 rounds [of small arms ammunition] *per man only, but no ammunition for officers' revolvers. We had no picks or shovels, grenade, mines, wire or medical appliances; not had we any means of communication within the company in the form of wireless sets.*

During the morning of 22 May Captain Bickford received instructions to proceed to St-Omer:

I left Don at about 2.00pm and arrived at the area Fort Rouge, where I took the Royal Berkshire platoon down the road to the bridge at Arques ... I ordered the Berkshire platoon under PSM Dakin to hold this bridge and wrote him an authority for blowing it if necessary ... At about 8.00pm I had called up my remaining two platoons and we moved over the canal to St-Omer. There we found a detachment of searchlight personnel holding the bridge by the station. They had 3-ton lorries across the bridge as a road block (the bridge had not been prepared for demolition), and I immediately proceeded to take over the positions, as they stated they had had no sleep for two nights. Having no tools for digging, we were unable to construct any defences, and the men were obliged to take up positions as darkness came on by lying behind local obstacles.

At about 10.45pm a staff officer from Hazebrouck turned up and enquired as to the whereabouts of the armoured division that had landed at Calais earlier that day. Clearly referring to 3/RTR, he was unaware these vehicles were still in the process of being unloaded and of the circumstances regarding Calais and the 10th Panzer Division.

During the afternoon of 22 May the 9/Royal Northumberland Fusiliers were instructed to send X Company, under the command of 33-year-old Captain Ernest Hart, to the bridges between Blaringhem and St-Momelin, taking with them much of the battalion transport. We already know that he left No 6 Platoon under Second Lieutenant Ross at St-Momelin and then moved south with the remainder of his company to St-Omer. Taking the road on the west bank of the canal, Hart's men were apparently directed by French soldiers into what transpired to be an ambush. It is likely that

Lieutenant Colonel Lechmere Cay Thomas commanded the 9/Royal Northumberland Fusiliers.

these men were fifth columnists and after a short and sharp engagement all were taken prisoner. No mention is made of Hart's men in Bickford's report and it would appear that he was unaware of their demise. Captain Hart was shot by the Germans on 24 May as he was being marched into captivity; he is commemorated on the Dunkirk Memorial.

Back at the bridge, in between the intermittent shelling, Bickford sent out a patrol to report on the remaining two bridges in the town, which he subsequently discovered to be unmanned. Personally supervising the blocking of these bridges with whatever vehicles came to hand, he placed one section of Royal Army Service Corps personnel on each bridge. Hoping in vain that the situation could not deteriorate much more, he received news – incorrectly as it turned out – that the 52/Heavy Regiment at the St-Momelin bridge had withdrawn. Depleting his small force even further, he sent a platoon of Royal Welch Fusiliers to St-Momelin with instructions to defend the bridge. These men eventually withdrew with Lieutenant Colonel Comerford.

In the meantime, shortly after midnight, a searchlight regiment major arrived at the Railway station with orders to remove the three searchlight regiment vehicles that were on the bridge and insisted his drivers carry out their instructions immediately. Bickford had little choice but to comply and, after replacing the vehicles with his own transport, he must have wondered if his run of bad luck had ended. Unfortunately it had not and, as the shelling increased in intensity, reports were now coming in of German tanks in the town on the far side of the canal:

The road bridge leading to the railway station at St-Omer.

Quite a number of shells fell on the canal banks within 150 yards of our position and some hit the station buildings just behind us; but no one was hurt, and when daylight came, I took immediate steps to reorganize my positions. First of all I took all personnel off the bridge and arranged for it to be covered from a flank. I then ordered my one anti-tank rifle to occupy a shell hole position in the wall of a house on the other flank about 100 yards south of the bridge.

At about 6.30am on 24 May a French colonel and a staff officer arrived and promised to send up two tanks and an anti-tank gun. The gun arrived just as a German machine gun opened up from the far side of the bridge, the horse drawn limber with its ammunition bolted, leaving the gun useless. At the same moment the German attack began when an enemy tank appeared on the far side of the bridge:

It then withdrew, returning almost immediately with three others, and from the far bank, at a range of about seventy yards, they proceeded to plaster our positions with gun and machine gun fire. One of the first shells set our lorries on fire, and a column of smoke went up. The firing was intense and lasted until the lorries had almost burnt out, when the tanks proceeded to advance towards us across the bridge.

In the circumstances there was little Bickford could do but order his party to withdraw behind the railway station, from where they could hear the sound of firing coming from St-Momelin. With every man fending for himself, they withdrew across the flat countryside, reaching Bergues on 25 May.

German infantry advancing under fire.

Chapter Three

Polforce

Polforce was formed on 20 May and dissolved five days later on 25 May. For those five days it was under the command of 52-year-old Major General Henry 'Squeak' Curtis, who had been appointed to command the 46th Division in 1939. As a young officer, Curtis had arrived in France in December 1914 and concluded the First World War unscathed with the DSO and MC. He commanded the 1/King's Royal Rifle Corps (KRRC) from 1931–34 and although he was to survive the Second World War, his two sons were both killed: 20-year-old Lieutenant Phillip Curtis in November 1943, serving with the 2/KRRC in Italy and 22-year old Flight Lieutenant Richard Curtis in January 1944, while flying a Typhoon with 198 Squadron.

Dubbed Polforce, because it was intended St-Pol would host Curtis' HQ, his orders were to prevent German forces from crossing the line of canals running from Aire-sur-la-Lys (Aire) and La Bassée; shortly afterward this line was increased northwards to include Watten. On 23 May the line was increased again, this time by another fourteen miles to Râches to include part of the line previously defended by Macforce. It was an almost impossible task and one is reminded again of the Fifth Army line of defence in 1918, when their area of responsibility was continually extended, with disastrous consequences.

The orders received by Curtis on 20 May and signed by the Deputy Chief of the General Staff were quite specific:

You will take over command of Polforce. This force consists of:
(a) One 25-pounder battery, detailed by I Corps, and Brigade HQ and units of 46 Division at present en route by rail to the SECLIN area. These units detrain this afternoon at ST-POL where you will meet them and give them orders. They will be maintained under arrangements made direct by you with Brigadier Greenslade at BRASSARD. Your role is to establish localities in ST-POL, FREVENT and DIVION. This force will place their locality in a state of anti-tank defence, ensuring that a keep is established at which posts on the roads can rally if necessary.
(b) You are also in command of the La Bassée Canal defences

37

between AIRE and exclusive CARVIN. On your left you will be in touch with MACFORCE whose HQ are in ORCHIES. Forces under your command will consist of 25 Infantry Brigade of 50 Division and certain RE Units, the detail of which you will obtain direct from the Engineer-in-Chief.

On paper the plan sounded good, although the promised battery of 25-pounder guns mentioned in paragraph (a) failed to arrive and, of the infantry units of 46th Division, only the 2/5 West Yorkshires actually detrained as the remaining battalions were caught up in the German advance on Abbeville and the Channel coast. Thus, with paragraph (a) entirely negated by the speed of the German advance, the units that came under the command of Polforce for the defence of the canal on 20 May were:

2/5 West Yorkshires, 137 Brigade
The three battalions of 25 Infantry Brigade
One troop from 74/Field Regiment RA
101, 216 and 228 Field Companies RE
61 and 62 Chemical Field Companies, RE
Twenty dispatch riders for the purposes of communication

Brigadier Gawthorpe and 137 Brigade
The 49-year-old Brigadier John Gawthorpe was commissioned into the West Yorkshire Regiment in 1911 and served through the First World War, rising to command the 7/Leeds Rifles in 1938. A year later he was recalled from retirement and appointed to command 137 Brigade, 46th (North Midland and West Riding) Division, arriving in France in April 1940. The 46th Division was a second line Territorial division and a duplicate of the 49th Division, which in May 1940 was fighting in Norway. Ordered to move north to join Polforce, the three trains containing the men of 137 Brigade were delayed by German bombing at Abbeville and only the train containing the 2/5 West Yorkshires and Brigade Headquarters managed to pass through unscathed before the Abbeville junction became impassable. Detraining at Béthune, the West Yorkshire battalion was deployed to defend the canal between the St-Venant-Lilliers road bridge and Hinges, a distance of some six miles, which for an untrained and poorly equipped battalion would have been almost laughable if the situation had not been so serious.

With his command reduced to one infantry battalion, Gawthorpe attended the conference at Polforce Headquarters on 21 May, where he was told the forward defended localities (FDLs) were to be held at all costs and that the chain of canals would be an obstacle to the German advance. Gawthorpe did not allow his doubts to override his professionalism but the inexperience of many of the units deployed to the defence of the canal must have given him several sleepless nights. Over the next two days various other units were deployed to strengthen Polforce. Brigadier Chadwick, commanding 2 Anti-Aircraft Brigade, took initial responsibility for the defence of the bridges between St-Omer and Watten and Lieutenant Colonel Ames, from 3/Survey Regiment RA, provided a more reliable communications network. Other units that were drafted in included 9/Royal Northumberland Fusiliers, the guns of 'A' Field Regiment, a battery of guns from 98/Field Regiment and the Don Details.

392/Battery, 98/Field Regiment (Surrey and Sussex Yeomanry)
The guns of 392/Battery were in action on the Escaut River when orders were received from GHQ on 20 May for one battery to proceed immediately to St-Pol and come under the orders of Brigadier Gawthorpe's 137 Brigade. [There are conflicting accounts in various sources as to whether the regiment was equipped with 18 or 25-pounders guns, however, the account written by Major Cubitt clearly states the 'regiment consisted of two batteries of 25-pounders'.]

A 25-pounder field gun of the type used by the gun crews of 392/Battery.

Leaving 391/Battery on the Escaut, Hon Charles Cubitt and the officers and men of 392 (Surrey) Battery departed with D, E and F Troops and eleven guns. Cubitt's visit to Gawthorpe at Morbecque Château highlighted the state of confusion and disarray that was prevalent at the time. Here he was told that 137 Brigade consisted of one anti-aircraft battery and a company of engineers, Brigade HQ had completely lost touch with their infantry and the only information available was that a few enemy tanks had broken through, quite where was unclear, and the intention was to hold the line of the canal until a, as yet unknown, division of infantry could arrive. To add to the overall confusion, once Cubitt had arrived back at his command post on 22 May, Lieutenant Colonel Edward Burns, commanding 'A' Field Regiment, arrived to inform him that 392/Battery was now under his command and the 'A' Field Regiment's guns would take over the crossings between Aire and Béthune, while 392/Battery would hold the line of the canal crossings between St-Momelin and Wittes inclusive, a distance of twelve miles. He was also informed that a battery of French 75s and five guns of a Belgian anti-tank battery would give them assistance. 'At least the Belgian battery turned up,' wrote a sceptical Cubitt, 'which is more than can be said of the French gunners.' The Belgians were positioned a mile north west of Lynde, covering the valley running between Renescure and Ebblinghem. Cubitt's report continued:

> *Everything went smoothly with one exception: the second gun of E troop, destined for the crossing at St-Omer, was stopped as it passed through Hazebrouck by a staff officer who ordered it into action on the outskirts of that town, in close defence of GHQ. Thus the St-Omer crossing was left without artillery defence. The remaining six guns moved into position during the night.*

At the time Cubitt had no idea the St-Omer gun (E2) had been redeployed and, quite naturally, having had no communication from the gun crew, thought the gun was in serious trouble and in need of support. In the opinion of the author the E2 gun would have served a greater need at St-Omer and, had Cubitt been informed of its deployment at Hazebrouck, Major Andrew Horsborough-Porter and his squadron of 12/Lancers armoured cars would not have had an unnecessary and rather dangerous foray into St-Omer to locate it. In the meantime, Major Cubitt deployed the guns from E and F Troops to strengthen the garrisons between St-Momelin and Wittes to cover the main crossing points on the canal and ordered the four remaining guns of D Troop to give covering fire along the whole frontage from a position just north of Ebblinghem.

The bridge at St-Momelin
The fight at St-Momelin has been dealt with in Chapter 2. When Second Lieutenant George Peile and the E1 gun crew turned up they came under the command of 52/Heavy Regiment; in fact the crew never rejoined

The 12/Lancers were equipped with CS9 Armoured Cars.

392/Battery and remained with Lieutenant Colonel Comerford's men for the remainder of the campaign and were evacuated from Dunkerque. The gun was brought briefly into action on 25 May against enemy machine guns before it was destroyed by the crew on orders from 52/Heavy Regiment.

The bridges at Arques

There is a note in the war diary of 5/Casualty Clearing Station (CCS) that on 21 May they were at the Château de Westhove on the northern edge of Blendecques, some three miles to the southwest of Arques. Major George McNab's diary relates an episode where, on returning from Renescure railway station in an ambulance, he was stopped at the road bridge and told it was about to be demolished. Having secured permission to cross and told he would be on the wrong side of the canal when the

The bridge at Arques as it looked in May 1940.

Germans arrived, he continued on his journey back to Blendecques, expecting, he writes in his diary, to be taken prisoner. Fortunately, the CCS personnel escaped the German advance and headed north to St-Omer.

On 22 May Captain Wilfred Bickford, commanding No 3 Company, Don Details, arrived at Arques where he found No 2 Section from 228/Field Company had blown the footbridge next to the main road bridge, which they had also prepared for demolition. In the process three men were killed and four were wounded in what appeared to have been a premature explosion. One of these men was Sapper Gordon Upton, whose name is commemorated on the Dunkirk Memorial. Deploying one of his platoons to hold the road bridge, the defences were reinforced at 7.30pm by the arrival of a detachment of 9/RNF, under the command of Second Lieutenant Dakin. Bickford writes that, before moving north to St-Omer, he deployed Dakin's men to hold the railway bridge. This may well be the case but, although the road bridge was destroyed by the 228/Field Company at 4.30am on 23 May, it is unclear what took place at the railway bridge. Bickford wrote in his report that the road bridge was blown just as German tanks 'came over the bridge' and one of the leading tanks went into the canal.

The E3 gun crew from 393/Battery withdrew with the sappers to report back to Major Cubitt for further instructions. Cubitt immediately ordered the gun to return, by which time the Germans were already in the village and the gun came into action at a crossroads about one mile east of Arques. Here some nineteen rounds were fired at the advancing Germans before the gun eventually rejoined D Troop at Morbecque; but not before Captain Greenwell was taken prisoner.

The 12/Lancers Reconnaisance

The five armoured cars that remained in Major Andrew Horsbrugh-Porter's A Squadron were instrumental in enabling the 392/Battery gun to retire intact from Arques on 23 May; but soon after leaving the canal side town they were despatched to Ebblinghem to support the withdrawal of Major Cubitt and D Troop, who were under severe pressure from enemy tanks. Lieutenant Tim Bishop was serving with A Squadron and recalled the attack as 'well and truly climbing out of the frying pan into the fire'. Suddenly, he wrote, he observed a German tank breezing along on a parallel road:

Lieutenant Tim Bishop.

I noticed it had a Nazi flag draped across it as aircraft recognition, scarlet and white in contrast to the bits of foliage that decorated our own vehicles in a touching attempt to camouflage them. Another big black-looking tank came swanning along, with an enviable lack of caution, to join the first, which had stopped. They were perhaps 400 yards away. I was willing them not to see us when Bruce [Lieutenant Bruce Shand] started rat-tatting with his Bren, pouring tracer bullets into a wood occupied by the enemy, on a bank the other side of the road from the tanks. The second tank traversed its gun so I loosed off at it with the Boys rifle and hit it on the side of the turret. For all the effect it had I might have been a little girl trying to hurt a heavyweight boxer.'

Bishop fired another round almost at the same time as it began to pour with rain, which thankfully masked his escape from the tank's retaliatory fire. Ordered to follow Horsbrugh-Porter and passing a British gun and its crew lying dead beside it, the squadron ran straight into a mass of German infantry:

Our squadron leader acted swiftly and saved us from total destruction. He unhesitatingly swung off up a muddy track and through a ploughed field yet to be sown ... The main lot of infantry were lining the headland, some wore helmets, others were bare headed. I got a quick impression of blonde, sullen boys, pink cheeked from the heavy rain. Their field grey uniforms looked dark and sodden ... The line of armoured cars coming round the corner must have been just as unpleasant for them as suddenly bumping into them had been for us.'

Sadly, Second Lieutenant Andrew Roddick was killed and Major Lord Erne, the second in command, later died of his wounds. However, Cubitt's guns of D Troop had been saved and Andrew Horsbrugh-Porter was awarded the DSO, an award that Tim Bishop heartily endorsed in his diary. 'If the knocked out gun we had passed earlier was on the right flank of the battery position, then the guns would indeed have been captured.' Bishop, the son of Lieutenant Colonel Harry Bishop, who commanded 1/Lancashire Fusiliers at Gallipoli in 1915, survived the war, as did Andrew Horsbrugh-Porter.

The bridge at Renescure
The bridge was just over a mile west of Renescure and is referred to in some sources at the bridge at Campagne. The rather meagre garrison was reinforced by 6/Battery from 2/Searchlight Regiment on 22 May and the E4 gun from 392/Battery, which was positioned about 200 yards east of the bridge. At what time the sappers from 58/Chemical Warfare Company (CWC) arrived is unclear, but Blaxland suggests it was at dawn on 23 May. Under the command of Major Ifan Lloyd, the sappers found the Germans dismantling a barricade on the far side of the bridge and at once mounted an attack and pushed a truck loaded with explosive onto the bridge. The detonation failed to break the back of the bridge but did at least deter any further infantry incursion for much of the day. 58/CWC was one element of the 1/Chemical Warfare Group and was initially held in GHQ Reserve along with 61 and 62/CWCs. A Chemical Warfare Company consisted of an HQ and three sections, each of three sub-sections, equipped with thirty Livens Gas Projectors and organized in such a way that it could quickly assume the more traditional role of an RE field company. The Livens Projector was a crude but effective First World War vintage mortar, capable of throwing a thirty-pound canister some 1000 yards.

At 8.30am small arms fire developed into heavy mortar fire being directed from the houses opposite the partly demolished bridge. Opening fire, the E4 gun destroyed two of the houses on the opposite bank at the cost of two of the gun crew being wounded. An enemy armoured vehicle was destroyed before the gun came under heavy mortar fire around 4.00pm and the crew were forced to take cover. The attempt to recover the gun was foiled when enemy fire broke the tractor axle, the position

The Château de Zuthove at Rensecure.

was overrun and the gun abandoned. It was during this withdrawal that Driver Albert Hardy from 58/CWC was awarded the Military Medal. Realizing two men from the party were missing, he returned to his former headquarters at Château de Zuthove to find it deserted. Returning to his company under heavy fire, he continued to nurse his vehicle to Dunkerque and eventual evacuation.

The counter-attack of 24 May

It was not until late on 23 May that Brigadier Gawthorpe finally mustered enough troops to mount a counter attack in an attempt to delay the German advance from Aire. It was launched at dawn on 24 May by a mixed body of troops from 5/Royal Inniskilling Dragoon Guards, C Squadron, 4/7 Royal Dragoon Guards, 9/RNF and the guns of 57 (East Surrey) Anti-Tank Regiment. The attack caught the German armoured column by surprise and the ensuing battle not only held up the German advance, but destroyed several of its armoured vehicles. Captain Phillip Hampton, commanding the 57/Anti-Tank Regiment's 228/Battery, recalled the occasion vividly:

45

There were German tanks practically stopped, shooting like fury. Our guns had arrived just in time and we were taking them on – we were giving them shot for shot – two German tanks were caught and blew up in a great sheet of flame and clouds of smoke. A British tank suffered a similar fate – there were about eight German tanks there.

The British tank referred to may have been from 4/7 Royal Dragoon Guards, as they reported one tank knocked out and its commander killed. Captain Hampton was awarded the MC.

Captain Phillip Hammond, 57/Anti-Tank Regiment.

The bridge at Wardrecques

The F1 gun from 393/Battery was in support of French infantry holding the bridge, which was east of the village. The 2/Searchlight war diary says that Lieutenant Doll, commanding a party from 6/Battery, ordered the bridge to be blown just after 7.00am on 23 May. By 8.30am the gun was in action, shooting by direct fire, and occasionally by the observed fire of a French officer. The enemy machine gun on the opposite bank

German engineers were adept at throwing up temporary bridges across the canal. This picture was taken on 15 May 1940 at a crossing point on the Meuse and shows French prisoners being escorted across.

was put out of action but the retaliatory mortar fire killed the French officer and forced the detachment to abandon its position by 11.00am. Sergeant James, commanding the gun crew, was saved the necessity of disabling the gun after a direct hit by a German mortar. The 6/Battery war diary goes on to say that Lieutenant Doll, one captain and five sappers, together with four men of the 9/RNF, withdrew at 1.30pm to Bergues. It is possible that Doll confused the men of 392/Battery with what he thought were men from the RNF, as there is no record of the 9/RNF being deployed to the bridge.

The bridge at Blaringhem

The crossing was defended by some 200 French infantry, a searchlight detachment from 2/Searchlight Regiment under Second Lieutenant Groombridge and some Royal Army Ordinance Corps personnel. In many ways this was the most successful action carried out by 392/Battery, as during the first attack, which occurred at about 8.30am, the F2 gun scored direct hits on one tank and two other armoured vehicles. At 11.00am a second and heavier attack was launched, leaving only the 392/Battery gun in action under the direction of Second Lieutenant Kenneth Payne. Shooting over open sights, Payne's gun fired no less than 130 rounds into the advancing enemy, withdrawing only when the gun came within hand grenade range:

The temporary bridge at Blaringhem is another example of the work of German engineers.

Under the very noses of the enemy the gun was limbered up and might well have got away had not an unlucky shell from a German tank severed the engine connector as the party pulled out of the position. The gun was lost.

Second Lieutenant Groombridge was badly injured and several of his men were killed when German units forced a passage across the canal using some of the sunken barges. A rear defence line was formed temporarily at Lynde until they were dispersed under a heavy German bombardment. Payne got his party away and was awarded an MC for his conduct during the action.

The bridge at Wittes
The bridge at Wittes referred to in the 1940 literature was actually at Garlinghem, which is just south of the current road bridge. The crossing was initially held by a unit from 127 Brigade, which were part of Macforce, until it was withdrawn on 21 May. No longer in existence, the bridge was prepared for demolition by HQ Section, 228/Field Company on 20 May. At about 2.00pm on 22 May a premature explosion took place, demolishing the bridge and killing 25-year-old Captain Wilfred Middleton and Sapper Joseph Huntington. Sapper Cyril Moreland died of wounds the next day. All three men are buried in Aire Communal Cemetery. The F3 Gun from 392/Battery was deployed here to hold the crossing but communication was lost and, as discovered later, the detachment were taken prisoner.

The bridges at Aire-sur-la-Lys
Aire-sur-la-Lys (Aire) is at the junction of the Canal d'Aire with the canalised River Lys, which heads east towards St-Venant and Merville. There is a degree of uncertainty as to exactly which BEF units were defending the Aire bridgeheads, but we do know that 228/Field Company prepared and destroyed three bridges here and there was a considerable French presence in the town, west of the canal. The 228/Field Company war diary also records an attack by German aircraft on the RAF petrol dump and a French military train, which was in the railway station. Direct hits created large fires and explosions and petrol and ammunition continued to explode intermittently for some time afterwards. At 8.00pm, fearing the Germans would attempt to cross the canal, 228/Field Company blew the main road bridges, leaving the foot bridges intact. Brigadier Gawthorpe writes that he was at Aire on 23 May and discovered the French garrison was in the act of withdrawing:

Aire-sur-la-Lys hosts the junction with the Lys Canal. This bridge at the Bassin des Quatre Faces controls the flow of water into the town.

The French commander informed me he had orders to rejoin his corps. As he had been properly placed under British command I ordered him to remain in position until such a time as regular instructions came through British HQ. Then I proceeded to check stragglers and to site a series of secondary positions for stragglers to be posted. These now included some British from posts adjoining the French ... finding a British major and French officer we handed over these partly occupied positions to them for the moment and, though the withdrawal was checked, but [sic] the whole of the French troops withdrew during the night.

The British major was probably Major A J Page, commanding 228/Field Company, as his citation for the MC recognizes that he was responsible for 'rallying British and French troops for a defence of the bridgeheads'.

It would appear that 228/Field Company also took over the responsibility from the French for the railway bridge at Isbergues, which was demolished later on 23 May, after the British sappers assisted wounded French personnel to cross the canal, casualties from the tank battles at Aire and St-Hilaire-Cottes with units from the SS-*Der Führer* Regiment. 228/Field Company were responsible not only for blowing the bridges at Aire and Garlinghem (Wittes) but also at Thiennes. They apparently prepared the bridges at Arques but, according to some sources, they were later blown by 101/Field Company.

Clearly, by 24 May, German units were across the canal, as Lieutenant Cecil Blacker of the 5/Royal Inniskilling Dragoon Guards recalls mounting a counter attack to take the pressure from the 9/Royal Northumberland Fusiliers, who were almost surrounded by German armoured vehicles near Boeseghem:

We were ordered to counter attack and **Lieutenant Cecil Blacker,**
extricate them. C Squadron, with a squadron **taken after the war.**
of 13/18 Hussars, were ordered to advance
under cover given by the artillery. They were to advance to
Boeseghem and somehow keep the Germans occupied so as to
permit the infantry to slip away. The attack was successful and
had the effect of releasing a large number of German tanks from
Boeseghem.

Not all the Northumberland Fusiliers got away, the battalion war diary noting that Second Lieutenant Hook and 2 Platoon from W Company were taken prisoner on the Boeseghem to Aire road:

Accompanied by Captain Ainsley [the platoon] *was forced to take*
up a position in a farm where it was subjected to heavy machine
gun fire and mortar fire, but managed to maintain its position –
assisted by flanking fire from the reserve platoon ... At 1.00pm
orders were received to withdraw to Steenbecque, which was
completed except for 2/Lt Hook's platoon, which, having got out
of the farm, was last seen in a ditch by the road.

While Hook and his men were taken prisoner, Captain Ainsley appears to have escaped unscathed, thanks to the efforts of the Royal Inniskilling Dragoon Guards.

That afternoon Polforce headquarters received a message from Général Georges-Edgar Boucher, commanding the French 5th Motorized Infantry Division, that their posts east of Aire, from Isbergues to Guarbecque, had been overrun and the division could take no further part on the defence of the canal. For Gawthorpe the news was devastating, as a sector of the southern flank of the Canal Line was now wide open to the German advance unless it could be stopped.

German troops on the march.

The 2/5 West Yorkshire Regiment

Apart from a rifle and bayonet per man, the five hundred officers and men of the 2/5 West Yorkshires (137 Brigade) were only armed with ten Bren guns and eleven Boys rifles; quite what Brigadier Gawthorpe expected of them in the event of a German advance across the canal is anyone's guess. He must have hoped that the canal would be an effective anti-tank ditch, providing, of course, that the bridges were destroyed. But as every soldier knows, unless bridges are completely demolished, determined infantry will always find a way to cross using the destroyed superstructure.

The blame for much of their eventual demise, and indeed that of the 2/5 Leicesters on the Deûle Canal, has been placed at the feet of Major General Curtis, who rashly argued that the 46th Division was ready and able to take its place as a front line fighting force. What possessed him to make this claim is unclear but his offer was apparently seized upon by a beleaguered BEF and the West Yorkshires and Leicesters found themselves facing the might of the German armoured divisions on the canal. Curtis may well be partly responsible; but the strategic situation that was unfolding around the BEF would have inevitably drawn in any unit that was remotely able to hold a position long enough to delay the German advance.

51

Apart from their rifles, the poorly armed and equipped 2/5 West Yorkshires only had Bren guns and Boys rifles with which to stop the German advance.

Commanded by Lieutenant Colonel Edward Pulleyn, the West Yorkshires took up defensive positions between the l'Epinette road bridge on the St-Venant-Lilliers road to the Hinges road bridge at la Combarderie. Dawn on 22 May saw all five companies deployed along the six mile frontage and Battalion Headquarters established near Robecq, on the D69 Calonne road. That evening Pulleyn made his final deployments, with HQ Company on the right flank, B Company in the centre and C Company covering the left flank up to, and including, the Hinges road bridge. Held in support were A and B Companies. Firing was heard coming from the direction of Guarbecque during the night of 22 May and Pulleyn ordered the bridges to be blown. There was one casualty in D Company; 34-year-old Private Robert Fenwick was hit by flying masonry and became the battalion's first fatality. He is buried in Robecq Communal Cemetery.

German movement towards the canal was confirmed just after dawn on 23 May by Lieutenant McLean of HQ Company, who practically bumped into the Germans in the village of Busnes, evidence that was supported later in the afternoon by an enemy armoured fighting vehicle approaching the l'Epinette bridge, opposite the HQ Company. The AFVs appearance heralded the arrival of an armoured column which, after advancing towards the British positions, opened a heavy barrage of mortar fire on the unfortunate West Yorkshires. At the same time, the French units from the French 5th Motorized Division, who were holding the partly demolished railway bridge at Guardbecque, came under heavy fire but, unlike the West Yorkshires, who remained in their trenches, they withdrew, to be followed by German infantry clambering over the remains of the bridge. As the French units pulled back, the gap in the line between Guarbecque and the 2/5 West Yorkshires was quickly exploited by the SS-*Verfügungs* Division, with HQ Company finding themselves in great danger of being outflanked. This rather unwelcome turn of events left them little choice but to withdraw to a new line along the road between Robecq and Calonne.

X and Y Force

Two further *ad hoc* forces were created on 23 May, both designed to form a temporary defence line along the canal ahead of the infantry, who were en-route from the Escaut and, apart from the odd reference in contemporary war diaries, very little is known of the operational movements of either force. The first of these was commanded by Brigadier Charles Findlay, the 2nd Division CRA, and designated Y-Force, although it was also known as Finforce. Findlay's force was made up of 13/Anti-Tank Regiment and 16/Field Regiment, together with the 6/Argyll and Sutherland Highlanders from I Corps reserve. Finforce removed almost half of the 2nd Division's artillery from divisional command, and it appears to have been disbanded on 25 May; 16/Field Regiment war diary reporting it was reassigned to the 46th Division. Findlay, it appears, was 'propped up' by Lieutenant Colonel Francis Watson, the CO of 99/Field Regiment, and passed over once he had returned to the UK.

In command of X-Force was Brigadier the Hon Edward 'Fred' Lawson, the CRA of the 48th Division; his force consisted of a company of machine gunners, the 18-pounders of 68(South Midland) Field Regiment, 9/Field Company, RE and an anti-tank battery. The 68/Field Regiment war diary refers to 'Lawson's Force' as being a mobile force 'that was to stem the advance of an enemy unit thought to be penetrating NW to the channel ports'. A tall order indeed! Lawson later wrote that Charles Findlay and

Brigadier the Hon Edward Lawson.

53

he only had a rather vague idea of what they were supposed to do and none whatever of the relative importance in the general scheme of things:

> *He* [Findlay] *must have been warned I was roving in the neighbourhood because he told me I was commanding X-Force, which was news to me. Naming forces after individual commanders or by letters is the first sign of the dissolution in an army. If I had known then what I learned since about these shot-gun christenings, I should have felt unhappy.*

A former CO of 99/Field Regiment, Lawson deployed 68/Field Regiment to le Touret on the D171, Regimental HQ was established a little further north in a farm house at Rue du Bas Chemin. The regiment's guns came into action on the afternoon of 24 May, firing on enemy concentrations around Béthune, until they were ordered to move to la Cordonnerie at 4.00pm on 25 May. Lawson later played an important part in the defence of the Dunkerque perimeter. He succeeded his father as 4th Baron Burnham in June 1943.

Chapter Four

25 Brigade

The three battalions of 25 Brigade were under the command of 52-year-old Brigadier William Ramsden. Commissioned into the West India Regiment in 1910, he served during First World War in the Cameroons and in Nigeria and then, from 1916, as a captain in the East Yorkshire Regiment, in France and Belgium. In 1936 he was appointed to command the 1/Hampshire Regiment, before rising to the rank of Brigadier and command of 25 Brigade. The brigade was an independent brigade and originally joined the lines of communications troops on its arrival in France in November 1939. In early May 1940 the brigade joined the 50th (Northumbrian) Division. Yet, between arriving at the canal and the Dunkerque evacuation, it was variously assigned to a succession of infantry divisions, causing some irritation amongst battalion commanders who were, at times, unsure of which division they were attached to. On 23 May the brigade became part of Polforce and was given the task of holding Béthune and the six miles of canal linking Béthune with La Bassée. Three days later, the 1/7 Queen's historian wrote that on the morning of 26 May 25 Brigade was definitely placed under the orders of the 2nd Division, but for a short time there 'seemed to be some doubt as to what formation actually commanded the 25th Brigade'.

Royal Irish Fusiliers digging anti-tank ditches at Nomain in February 1940.

1/Royal Irish Fusiliers

The battalion was under the command of 47-year-old Lieutenant Colonel Guy Gough and were assigned a frontage of just over six miles, running from the bridge at Avelette to Pont Fixe on the D166 Festubert – Cuinchy road. Gough came from an illustrious military family, three of whom had been awarded the Victoria Cross, and was commissioned into the 1/RIF four days after the outbreak of war in 1914. Fifteen days after being appointed to command the battalion, Gough and his men arrived on the canal shortly after first light on 21 May.

Lieutenant Colonel Guy Gough, commanding 1/RIF.

Gough quickly recognised the sector he had been allocated was far from ideal. A large section of the canal banks were raised as much as six feet above the surrounding countryside and, although there was some cover in the form of buildings and vegetation, other places were completely devoid of cover. Quite rightly, he decided to avoid defending the loop in the canal that ran through the northern suburbs of Béthune, and concentrated his defence on the line of the canal. He also recognized the most dangerous part of his frontage was on the right flank, with the bridge and lock at Avelette providing 'an open backdoor to our position'. The Royal Norfolk's war diary records the temporary absence of two companies who were reportedly lost until they were reunited with their battalion. The gap on the right of the RIF was apparently plugged with pioneers from the Norfolk's HQ Company. It could only have been this unit that caused Guy Gough to lose sleep over his right flank.

Once Gough's initial reconnaissance had been completed, he set about deploying his companies. In placing Second Lieutenant Sir Anthony 'Tony' Twysden and 13 Platoon, C Company, on the extreme right, astride the bridge

Second Lieutenant Sir Anthony Twysden (left) standing next to Second Lieutenant Charles O'Farrel, with Lieutenant Peter Murphy, commanding A Company, seated in front of them.

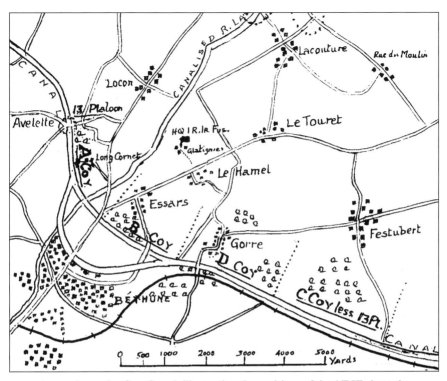

A map drawn by Guy Gough illustrating the positions of the 1/RIF along the canal.

at Avelette, he must have wondered if the 22-year-old baronet would survive the forthcoming encounter. Lieutenant John Horsfall writes that 13 Platoon 'had to hold a thousand yards of closed-in countryside, the two water courses that flanked it and the canal locks at Avelette, which, in the absence of bridges, provided the obvious first crossing point to our adversaries'. A Company was now under Second Lieutenant Claude Barrington [Captain Peter Murphy had been evacuated]. They held the ground up to the bridge on the Béthune-Estaires road, along with a composite company. B Company was commanded by Captain Quentin Findlater, whose sector ran from the bridge on the Béthune-Essars road to the canal junction west of Gorre. D Company, under Lieutenant John Horsfall, were on the right of B Company and held Gorre and the canal up to the junction at les Chantieres, while C Company was on the extreme left and under the command Lieutenant George Garside. Their sector ran up to Pont Fixe, west of Cuinchy, their left flank positions being in touch with 1/7 Queen's Royal Regiment (1/7 Queen's). Battalion Headquarters

57

The 1/RIF marching behind the battalion's band. The photograph was probably taken on the Belgian frontier before 10 May 1940.

was established at les Glattignies, a farmstead near le Hamel, on the D171 Essars–le Touret road.

The Composite Company

The composite company referred to by Gough was Number 4 Company of the Don Details, under the command of Lieutenant Graham Hoar, 1/Cameron Highlanders. His men, a mixed group of 6/Argyll and Sutherland Highlanders, RASC, 4/Royal Dragoon Guards and Royal Engineers, were about eighty strong and positioned in the A Company sector in front of Long Cornet, with instructions to hold as long as possible. Hoar wrote that French troops were along the canal bank at about 100 yard intervals, but over the next 36 hours they withdrew, leaving the composite company to face heavy German mortar attacks and the complete loss of a patrol 'killed to a man'. On 26 May, Hoar lost contact with the RIF and writes that they were machine gunned from the rear [presumably the result of 13 Platoon being overwhelmed] and, with the situation looking decidedly unhealthy, he decided to withdraw. Shortly after this Lieutenant Hoar was wounded and taken prisoner.

Gough's initial reconnaissance revealed hundreds of barges which, in places, were packed so tightly together that one could almost cross the canal without getting wet. His worry, that their presence would neutralize the effect of the canal as an obstacle, was shared by the 1/7 Queen's on his left and the 2/Essex on the Deûle Canal. Over the next day or so these barges were systematically destroyed, a task that Gough admits was heartbreaking, as 'we were destroying the homes, the stock-in-trade and the household goods of the bargees'.

As expected, the 7th Panzer Division's assaults were focused on the bridging points along the canal and although several of these had been destroyed by 22 May, a further four road bridges and a footbridge were not destroyed until forty eight hours later, possibly prompted by enemy attempts to rush the road bridge at Béthune on the B Company front. 'They were stopped short in their tracks', wrote Gough, 'with very heavy casualties by withering fire from 11 Platoon.' The bridge was blown during the second assault. It was this bridge that was also defended by two guns from 'A' Field Regiment; Lieutenant Colonel Burns writes of the 'very gallant action by Second Lieutenant Charles Kay-Shuttleworth and Acting Sergeant Turner'.

Gough summarized the action involving his battalion as having several phases, the first and second of which he described as spreading from his right flank:

Barges proved to be a headache for the 25 Brigade battalions as even when sunk they offered convenient bridging points across the canal.

Contact [with the enemy] *spread from the right of A Company, through B Company, to the right of D Company between about 2.00am and 10.30am on 24 May. By the latter hour, all platoons of both A and B Companies had been engaged. The fighting then spread left handed, until the whole of D Company was engaged. It increased in intensity as the enemy pressed to reach the canal piecemeal at various places at various times ... The net result of the thirteen hours fighting was as follows: our front was still intact, except perhaps on, or just beyond, the extreme right of D Company, where a small party of the enemy had probably got across the canal, but remained passive. We had suffered only about thirty-five casualties, and had inflicted an altogether disproportionately high number on the enemy.*

D Company had three road bridges in its sector of canal, which ran east from the junction at les Champs Boucquet. The 24-year-old John Horsfall, despite his age and relative inexperience, was to demonstrate a skill and tenacity on the canal that would earn him the MC and no doubt contributed to his rise to battalion command in the Irish Brigade in 1944. Horsfall's account mentions that on 21 May they were joined by a small body of French regulars, who arrived under an *adjutant chef*:

Lieutenant John Horsfall, commanding D Company.

They were armed to the teeth with [ammunition] *bandoliers slung round them, and they had a number of German weapons, including automatics. Most of them had bottles protruding from battle jacket pockets, and the overall impression was that of a party of pirates out on a shore raid. The chef came up to me and saluted. He paused for a moment of two, just looking me over, and then enquired what my instructions might be.* [Horsfall explained in French that his instructions were to defend the canal and that is what he intended to do.] *The chef grinned. He said that in that case he and his men would stay too – and that we could count on them.*

From Horsfall's description of the battle it appeared that this group never once attempted to seek real cover or dig in but remained defiant and, despite their heavy casualties, fought alongside his men. 'They made sure that no one of either army present at Gorre on 24 May 1940 would ever forget them. Certainly I never will.'

By mid morning on 24 May the weakness of Horsfall's 18 Platoon became evident when their positions were located by the enemy:

PSM Sidney Kirkpatrick's positions gradually became untenable as the enemy pinpointed them, and they were gradually shot to bits. He was hit himself about midday but, although incapacitated, he held on until nightfall, saying nothing in the meantime. Connolly had already been killed and his number 2 wounded. Kirkpatrick had taken over the Bren and was still in action with it, with the assistance of Fusilier Wilson, when the run of luck ended for both of them. As the blast from the Spandau came through the place, their gun was wrecked, Wilson lay dead and Sidney had a bullet through the shoulder with another that ripped down the side of his leg and had stripped off his gaiter buckles.

In the space of an hour 18 Platoon had lost eight men and had been reduced to only one working Bren gun.

A Company

On the A Company front German mortars and machine gun fire attempted to mask several attempts by the enemy to cross the canal. Barrington's men suffered ten casualties in this opening skirmish and many of these were on the left flank, where hostile mortar fire appeared to be at its heaviest. One particularly annoying machine gun, which was firing from the upper floor of a warehouse, was dealt with very efficiently by one of Major Collett-White's guns from 259/Anti-Tank Battery:

With two rounds from a 2-pounder he permanently dislodged the machine gun and its crew, and probably destroyed them. This was very fine shooting. The 2-pounder shell cut into the concrete and tore holes in it as if it were so much match boarding.

The Royal Irish Fusiliers faced Rommel's 7th Armoured Division on the far side of the canal.

Known amongst his men as 'High Explosive', Harold Edwin Collett-White's parent unit was 65/Anti-Tank Regiment, but over the course of the battle for France the various batteries often found themselves attached to other formations and units in a supporting role. Guy Gough writes warmly of Collett-White's contribution to the defence of the canal in his sector, remarking of 'the grand support and help his battery gave us in spirit as well as materially throughout the battle'. Late in the same

61

afternoon a small column of German tanks and motorcyclists attempted to cross the canal at Avelette but was checked by 13 Platoon and two guns from 25 Brigade Anti-Tank Company. From Gough's account it then appears that the enemy withdrew under fire but returned the next day, capturing the survivors, including Tony Twysden, who was badly wounded. Gough's initial fears for 13 Platoon had been realized. Twysden spent the remainder of the war in a German hospital and died a few months after returning home in 1945.

The battle intensifies
On 25 May enemy artillery units were brought into play. Horsfall admits that had the enemy been allowed to form any sort of front along the opposite bank of the canal they would have swept across the water in strength. From the very beginning the Irish marksmen and the supporting artillery units held the upper hand over their German counterparts by dispersing any attempts to cross the narrow stretch of water that divided the two sides. Opposite the 17 Platoon positions was a large goods yard that still contained a number of loaded railway wagons. Apart from providing cover for the Germans, what Horsfall's men were not aware of was the wagons were filled with French ammunition. A salvo from the Irish finally detonated the ammunition, which resulted in an unexpected 'prolonged series of explosions and a pyrotechnic display that was uncomfortable for 17 Platoon but quite lethal for the enemy'.

In the early hours of the 26th the 1/8 Lancashire Fusiliers from 4 Brigade, described by Gough as a 'stout-hearted but inexperienced battalion', began their relief of the battalion and, through no fault of their own, were thrown into an already deteriorating situation. Moving forward under severe shellfire, the Irish Fusiliers disengaged and headed north towards la Croix Rouge. We will look at the fortunes of the Lancashire Fusiliers in Chapter 7.

1/7 Queen's Royal Regiment
Described by Guy Gough as 'first rate comrades in arms', the battalion was allocated a 6,000 yard sector of the canal running from Givenchy to Salomé and was under the command of 44-year-old Lieutenant Colonel Gerald Pilleau. He joined the 1/Queen's Royal West Surreys in France in May 1915, a battalion which had been commanded by his uncle, Henry Pilleau, before his death

Lieutenant Colonel Arthur Pilleau commanded the 1/7 Queens.

on the Aisne in October 1914. Gerald Pilleau's father, a major serving with the 1/Hampshires, was killed a year later in Gallipoli. Carrying on the family military tradition, Gerald was appointed to command the 1/7 Queen's in February 1940, remaining in post until April 1941, when he was promoted to command 197 Infantry Brigade.

Despite two parties of men from A and C Companies being missing, the battalion arrived on the right flank of the RIF at 4.40am on 21 May, establishing Battalion HQ at Violaines. There were four main crossing points in the battalion sector: two bridges in the Givenchy sector, which was garrisoned by B Company and some of A Company; and the road and railway bridges at La Bassée in D Company's sector. The Queen's historian points out there was very little artillery support, but the guns that arrived at Givenchy bridge and fought 'without sights in an anti-tank role' were undoubtedly from 'A' Field Regiment who, Sir Martin Farndale reports in his *History of the Royal Regiment of Artillery*, were 'fighting with sights made from cardboard and old coat hangers'.

Company frontages were thinly held and the inevitable gaps in the line were covered by fighting patrols.

> *This patrolling was weird work, especially through the deserted streets of La Bassée. No enemy were ever encountered, but there were fifth column snipers lying up, who fired at isolated cars and dispatch riders ... Food was a big problem as no rations were coming up and the area had been cleared of civil supplies. Refugees were still streaming across the front in both directions, not knowing which way to go. Orders were that no one was allowed to cross the canal, so the wretched refugees had several times to be driven off the parked barges with the bayonet, a heart-rending task.*

On 23 May the missing parties from A and C Companies turned up and were dispatched to strengthen Major Ronald Senior's D Company and

A map from the *History of the Queen's Royal Regiment*, depicting the positions of the three 25 Brigade battalions on the canal and the approximate locations of the 1/7 Queen's companies.

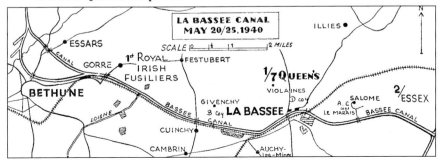

take over from the 2/Essex at Salomé, where a concrete footbridge crossed the canal. Senior would eventually become commanding officer of the battalion in October 1942 at El Alamein, before being promoted to command of 151Brigade. On the night of 25/26 the battalion was relieved on the canal by 1/Queen's Own Cameron Highlanders from 5 Brigade.

2/Essex Regiment

Under the command of Lieutenant Colonel Alexander Blest, the battalion arrived in France in September 1939 and was immediately employed on pioneer duties. On 23 April orders were received to join 25 Infantry Brigade and the battalion moved into Belgium on 10 May. With the retreat from the River Dyle underway, the battalion was placed under the orders of the 4th Division on 15 May and ordered to defend the bridges over the Charleroi Canal at Brussels; it was a short lived attachment as three days later they were again under 25 Brigade orders, this time with a new commanding officer. Lieutenant Colonel Blest, whose injuries from a car accident were turning septic, was replaced by Major Clifford Wilson. Orders to proceed directly to the La Bassée Canal arrived on 20 May, a journey that Private Treleaven considered to be rather tedious:

> *And so, in accordance with orders, the battalion embussed at 11.00pm at Belleghem, and was routed via Tournai-Lille-Seclin to Don, where it arrived at 6.00am, the 21 May, after a tedious and much-intermixed journey. This series of night moves with no lights was by now placing a heavy strain on the MT drivers, who were getting very tired. At Con, the 2nd Essex was once again ordered to take up defensive positions at the bridges over the Haute Deûle and La Bassée Canals with Battalion Headquarters at Meurchin. The wheel had turned full circle and the battalion, greatly to their surprise, found themselves back where they had started their advance into Belgium.*

The battalion frontage ran for approximately four and a half miles and contained nine bridges. On the right flank, with two bridges to defend, was Captain John Cramphorn and A Company, who were in touch with the 1/7 Queen's at Salomé. Cramphorn went on to command A Company, 13/Parachute Regiment, and dropped near Ranville to secure and clear a landing zone for Horsa Gliders on 6 June 1944. Major Howell and D Company were allocated a frontage of about 1,000 yards, including one bridge south of Bauvin, while Captain Jones and B Company had a 2,000 yard sector around Meurchin, containing one railway and two road bridges. Finally, C Company, under Major 'Archie' Newbold, had 2,500 yards of the left flank containing three bridges and running from Pont-à-Vendin to Estevelles.

By 22 May it had become obvious to all that, even with the bridges destroyed, the barges, which were present in the canal, presented just as much danger and offered ready-made bridging points for German engineers to use when constructing their pontoon bridges. John Cramphorn wrote of his concern:

I was not alone, I know, about the pile up of barges in the canal. Even when the bridges should be down, they would make crossing the canal very easy. We got permission finally to burn such of them as we could. And a rare old blaze they made too.

Second Lieutenant Anthony Irwin, seen here wearing the ribbon of the Military Cross.

It was a problem experienced all along the 25 Brigade sector. 21-year-old Second Lieutenant Anthony Irwin, serving in C Company, felt they posed a huge threat to their defences:

They were particularly large, had been anchored side by side and, in some places, formed a bridge right across the canal. We had to sink them. But we had no gun cotton and all we could do was open the sea-cocks. Luckily the centre of the canal was deep and they disappeared from view.

During the afternoon of 23 May seven of the nine bridges were blown, leaving the road bridges at Meurchin and Pont-à-Vendin intact. It was just as well, as at 6.00pm that evening the first contact with enemy vehicles came on the A Company front, followed by a bombing attack on HQ Company and Pont-à-Vendin. Anthony Irwin was unsure who was responsible for the blowing up the ammunition train which had been sitting in the good's yard for the previous week:

There is some doubt as to whether it was the bombers who hit it or whether, under cover of their bombardment, some spy had set it off. What is certain is that the trucks started to explode. There were twenty-seven coaches, and all were filled with unprimed 75mm shells ... All through the night the air was filled with shells and shell cases, screaming, shrieking across the sky. I think I was never so scared. One shell came crashing through the roof of my headquarters and landed on my bed. Another hit the door of the building and slid across the room, hitting and stopping at the far wall. It is lucky they were not primed, had they been no man in C Company would have lived to see morning.

C Company's sector did not, according to Irwin, 'begin to get interesting' until 24 May, when a German motorcycle patrol was seen on the far bank of the canal:

Suddenly there was a burst of fire from my left-hand section. I raced down to see what was happening, and was just in time to see a Hun motorcycle combination go head-over-heels into the canal, with its crew of three all dead. Another was turning in the road when a shot from the anti-tank rifle knocked the engine out and into the lap of the man sitting in the sidecar. The other two leapt off and ran into the wood, dragging their pal with them. A third vehicle stopped in the corner and got a machine gun into action against us in double quick time. A long burst of bullets hit the wall by my head, and I got down quick. Then came the shot of the century. It was our anti-tank man again. With one shot he hit the gunner and knocked his head clean off his shoulders.

From across the canal they could hear the Germans 'crashing about in the wood' and put in a long burst of Bren gun fire to encourage them to run faster. On the road lay the wrecked motorcycles and a machine gun:

I shouted for volunteers and Barnes and Fox, two old soldiers with pretty grubby crime sheets and hearts of lions, ran up. We hopped into a small boat and rowed across the canal. We had a quick look into the wood but the Hun seemed to have fled. Fox then ran for the machine gun and I got some maps out of the motorcycle and a couple of boxes of ammunition; we rowed back like hell with the booty.

No sooner had they scrambled up the side of the canal when a German tank appeared on the far side and began blazing away at Irwin's platoon. 'Bullets at the rate of a thousand a minute plopped, skidded and screamed at our feet. Stewart behind the anti-tank rifle was shooting like a man possessed.' The tank then retired only to reappear pushing an anti-tank gun into position which opened fire at the very same moment as Stewart – the German gunner missed his target, smashing the brickwork behind Irvine, but Stewart's round went 'straight through the shield, hit the

A German motorcycle combination similar to that which was attacked by Irwin's platoon.

gunner and threw him spread-eagled onto the top of the tank'. Twenty rounds were put into the tank which, according to Irvine, 'looked like a colander by the time we had finished'.

When Irwin's MC was announced in October 1940 the regiment made much of the fact that not only was the young subaltern commanding the same platoon as his father had twenty five years earlier, but also that the decoration was the first to be awarded to the Essex Regiment. Many more were to follow over the next five years. Anthony Irwin's father was 48-year-old Brigadier Noel Irwin, then commanding the 2nd Division who, by way of coincidence, had also been the first officer in the regiment to receive the MC in the previous conflict. The young Irwin had a fractious relationship with his father, which together with a rather restless spirit, saw him taking part in the ill-fated Dakar Raid in September 1940, gaining his glider pilot's wings in 1943 and joining V Force in the Burmese Arakan.

Enemy activity continued through 25 May, with frequent sightings of German armoured vehicles being reported along the length of the battalion's sector, a few shots were fired and B Company reported at least one enemy soldier killed. It was becoming pretty obvious to all concerned that within the next few days a major German advance would take place along the canal, an event that would not involve the Essex as their orders to be relieved by 2/5 Leicesters arrived around lunchtime. John Cramphorn later wrote that, despite the relief taking place under fire, the company left their positions in good order and without casualties.

Chapter Five

The Leicesters on the Deûle Canal

The 2/Essex were relieved on 25 May by 2/5 Leicestershire, a Territorial battalion that arrived in France during April 1940 with 139 Brigade, 46th Division, for labouring and construction work. Now attached to Polforce, desperation had forced the transformation of Lieutenant Colonel Ken Ruddle's men from a labour battalion to a front line fighting force in the space of seventeen days! What exactly went through the minds of the battalion's senior officers is anyone's guess, but one thing was becoming abundantly clear: if a brigade in such a poor state of readiness as 139 Brigade was now needed on the front line, then the situation must indeed be serious. Even if one ignored the almost absence of military training,

Officers of the Leicestershire Regiment prior to embarking for France. Second from left is Captain Geoff Gee; Lieutenant Robert Sharp and Captain Sydney Brown are fifth and sixth from the left.

the lack of equipment raised huge doubts as to the effectiveness of the Leicesters:

> There were no 3-inch mortars, carriers, anti-tank guns or 2-inch mortars. Instead of the established one Bren gun per section and one anti-tank rifle to each platoon, there were only one Bren gun per platoon and one anti-tank rifle per company. The battalion was sadly deficient in transport, having only eight 15-cwt trucks, three 30-cwt trucks, the commanding officer's car and a water cart.

As part of what was essentially a division of labourers, the absence of any divisional artillery was not really a factor in the demise of the Leicesters, or indeed for 139 Brigade, as the 46th Division never operated in its entirety and 139 Brigade never went into action as a brigade formation. Although the lack of artillery has been cited in some quarters as an issue in the inability of the Leicesters to hold the advancing enemy forces, what was of far more importance to Ken Ruddle as he moved towards the canal was the non existence of any form of communication, apart from two dispatch riders.

8 Durham Light Infantry

With the Leicester's dispatched to positions along the Canal de la Deûle, the 8/DLI moved from Givenchy-lès-La Bassée to Carvin, where it was spent the night in the Bois d'Epinoy. Lieutenant Colonel Beart had been wounded during the action west of Arras at Warlus on 21 May, and command of the battalion was now in the capable hands of Major Ross McLaren. News of the German crossing of the canal on 26 May, together with the desperate request for support received from the French, prompted McLaren to sent Second Ian Lieutenant

Second Lieutenant Ian English.

English and the six remaining carriers of the Carrier Platoon in support of French troops in Carvin. No mention is made of the plight of the Leicesters along the canal; but the general confusion that existed at the time is illustrated by the orders received by McLaren an hour after English had departed, ordering the Durhams first to Ypres – the battalion had already marched to Camphin to await the troop carrying transport – and then, on orders from Major General Henry Curtis himself, they were to return and mount a counter attack on Carvin, which was apparently occupied by the enemy. Surmising that the Carrier Platoon and Second Lieutenant English had already been overwhelmed, McLaren's men were quick to move into the attack and were ready to advance some forty minutes after the receipt of orders.

Meanwhile, the Carrier Platoon dug in on the southern edge of Carvin. English recalled a half hearted French counter attack that appeared to dwindle away to nothing after it began to rain heavily. The DLI counter attack that began at 5.00pm arrived to find the town practically deserted and no Germans anywhere in sight. It quickly became obvious the rumours of an enemy occupation of Carvin were entirely false. It was the men of A Company who discovered the Carrier Platoon in action against scattered groups of German troops who had crossed the canal. Intermittent shellfire continued until after dark, until fresh orders resulted in the battalion withdrawing from Carvin to Steenvoorde.

The Leicesters' positions
The 2/5 Leicesters de-bussed at the Bois d'Epinoy, south east of Carvin, at 4.40am on 25 May and at 9.00am marched to their positions along the Canal de la Deûle. If contemporary accounts are correct then this was some hours before the 8/DLI arrived. The original battalion allocation was of some 7,000 yards stretching from Pont-à-Vendin to the bridge at Oignies, a sector that was later increased to include Salomé. Company dispositions, having been adjusted to include the new sector, were as follows: C Company took over the right flank at Salomé, B Company was placed in reserve, while A Company, along with HQ Company and D Company, extended along the canal, each company occupying roughly a quarter of the battalion front. By late that night the battalion was in position, occupying a series of relatively isolated posts along a front line of almost eight miles, which they shared with French, Senegalese and Moroccan troops. Company HQs were behind the canal and Advanced Battalion HQ was at Meurchin, Ken Ruddle preferring to be 'on the spot for liaising with the gunners and the French'.

The battalion did not have long to wait before they were engaged by the enemy. Ruddle wrote in his account that in the late afternoon of 25 May he received a message from HQ Company to the effect that one section had withdrawn, most of the French infantry had vanished and the company was under severe pressure:

> *I went forward to see the situation for myself and found the mortar and artillery fire intense but not much small arms fire. I decided to send two sections with Bren guns from B (Reserve) Company to help HQ Company. This was done and the OC B Company went forward and placed the sections. I went forward to this area again later in the evening and found things quieter, the withdrawn*

section had apparently returned, presumably to a better position, but we could not actually trace them.

The HQ Company sector ran from Pont Maudit on the Carvin-Lens road to the Pont-à-Vendin railway bridge. Lieutenant Robert Sharp and his platoon were at Pont Maudit, near the distillery, while PSM Holtham and Sergeant Sales were on either side of the railway bridge at Estevelles. PSM Simpson was on the eastern side of the railway bridge at Pont-à-Vendin. The German attack began at 2.00pm and spread along the canal frontage and Captain Sydney Brown, commanding HQ Company, writes that after Captain Geoff Gee arrived with two sections of reinforcements from B Company, he set off with Company Sergeant Major (CSM) Chambers to visit PSM Holtham:

> *It was about 11.00pm and pitch black, visibility being only about two yards. About halfway down I heard digging and as everything was quiet I imagined the remaining French had come back and were digging in there. We moved quietly towards them and did not realize they were Germans, in fact not until I had spoken to them in French and they stood up. It was then too late to get back as they were all round us and we were both taken prisoner. The only thing I could do was let out a yell that Germans were there and hope the section 100-150 yards behind us would hear.*

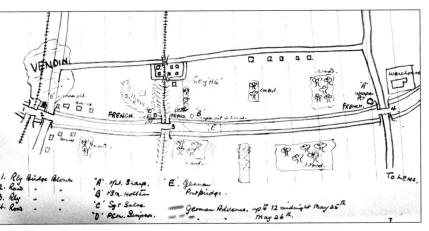

A map drawn by Captain Sydney Brown showing the position of HQ Company on the Deûle Canal.

The former railway embankment along which Captain Sydney Brown and CSM Chambers walked to visit the forward platoon positions located along the canal.

Brown writes that he walked along the railway embankment to the company positions on the canal, a walk that can be repeated today from Brown's former HQ Company headquarters, near Estevelles Communal Cemetery, along the now disused railway embankment. From Brown's account it becomes clear that units of the German 20th (Motorized) Infantry Division were preparing to advance en-mass across the canal on 26 May. Now a prisoner of war, he was able to watch the battle progress from the German line early the next morning:

> *At Dawn* [26 May] *I saw that about a whole battalion was over the canal. They already had two wireless sets working and also a field telephone working. Two of their mortars were working just near me and I watched them lobbing them down near where I had left Company HQ but could see none of our men.*

Lieutenant Robert Sharp at Pont Maudit was oblivious of Brown's capture and reported fighting throughout the morning of 26 May, with the enemy crossing on his right flank. At about 1.00pm German artillery ranged on the bridge, killing a few of the French; he writes that a *Capitaine* Thurbin then took charge and proposed they might be able to escape south under cover of darkness, a suggestion that came to nothing when enemy troops swept into the distillery yard at about 3.30pm. Sharp and his men surrendered on orders from Thurbin. Elsewhere on the HQ Company front isolated groups of men held out, but heavy machine gun and mortar fire steadily took its toll on the Leicesters; amongst the casualties was 22-year-old Second Lieutenant Hugh Pope, who was hit and died almost immediately. Others were more fortunate. Private George Arlott recalled the Germans arriving and, apart from being lined up against a wall in front of a machine gun – an episode that Arlott says concerned him a bit – the enemy soldiers were relatively civilized.

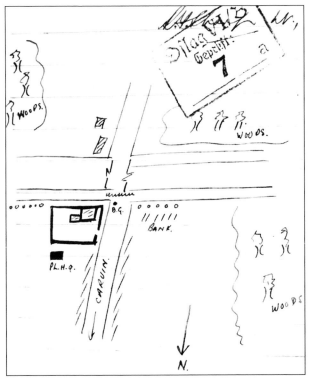

A map drawn by Lieutenant Robert Sharp depicting his position near Pont Maudit. Note the Stalag VIB stamp, indicating it had been drawn with permission from the camp commandant.

It was a similar story in the C Company sector; 20-year-old Second Lieutenant John Emerton was killed with 26-year-old Corporal Andrew Quigley, while firing one of the few Bren guns that the company had been issued with. Private Maurice Jennings recalled being billeted in a house on the canal overlooking a road bridge. After the two NCOs left with the Bren gun he writes that no one was left in charge of the remaining seven men. Armed with a rifle and five rounds of ammunition, he attempted to escape through the back door but was taken prisoner moments later. As the situation deteriorated, the remaining men of C Company, under the command of 47-year-old CSM Andrew Croxall, withdrew to the north, but their bid for freedom was to end the next day with captivity. Croxall, a First World War veteran, survived his imprisonment at Stalag XX-A at Thorn, during which time he was given news that his son, Anthony Croxall, had been killed serving with the 1/Leicesters in October 1944.

D Company, who were on the left flank just south of Oignies, had heard rumours to the effect that the Germans were across the canal on their right. Private Gordon Spring and his mates were armed with rifles, one Bren gun and an anti-tank rifle and dug in along the canal:

> I was at one end [of the trench] with the Bren gun and anti-tank rifle and we could see the German Panzers approaching and preparing to attack in a fork movement. We heard the Jerries had crossed the canal. I was sent to collect ammo and on my return I found the Jerries had crossed the canal near us and killed all the lads. I was on my own then. This was my baptism of fire. Imagine my stunned disbelief at what I saw. Mates, alive a few minutes ago, now lying dead, their gaping wounds making me feel sick.

Gordon Spring does not mention if he heard the sounds of the encounter which engulfed his mates or where he collected the ammunition from, but it does illustrate the speed at which the German units crossed the canal on 26 May. Another D Company soldier, Private Jim Hall, was in position near the road bridge north of Courrières:

> The bridge across the canal had been blown. It was just sagging in the middle. It was here I saw my first Germans. I was platoon runner at the time, so when the sergeant went on a recce, he took me with him. The Germans were on the other side of the canal amongst some factory buildings and we were on top of a railway embankment when I saw them. I remember I started jumping up and down like a bloody two year old ... The next thing I knew he had pushed me down the embankment saying 'get down you silly bugger'.

The railway bridge at Courrières in 1940.

Against all odds, both Hall and Spring survived their encounters and returned home via Dunkerque.

In the meantime, communication had been severed with Battalion HQ and, despite attempting unsuccessfully to get through to his company commanders, Ruddle wrote that they came under attack themselves:

> Very soon we were severely shelled and then dive bombers attacked us for over two hours. At the end of this there were no serious casualties, only a few minor wounds and some shell shock cases. Dispatch riders and others, who had been trying to get through to companies, brought rumours that the enemy had broken through and crossed the river in various places. No messages from companies, so tried again to get in touch. Owing to a lack of dispatch riders, long distances and continual shell fire, this proved impossible. The adjutant then went on a motor cycle to try and contact A Company but came back having had a bad crash, very shaken with damaged jaw and bleeding face etc.

The adjutant was Captain John Marshall, a regular officer who had been commissioned in 1936 into the 2nd Battalion. Evacuated via Dunkerque, he joined the newly raised airborne forces to fight in North Africa with

A coal mine pit head, not unlike the colliery on the southern edge of Carvin, where Captain Geoff Gee was positioned.

the 1st Airborne Division. After returning to the Leicestershire regiment after the war, he survived the Korean conflict only to drown whilst on holiday in Ireland.

Captain Geoff Gee and the remainder of B Company were positioned in a colliery on the southern edge of Carvin. Quite why there is no mention in the war diary of the 8/DLI remains unclear, but Lieutenant Richard Everard, who wrote of his experiences in *A Soldier's Tale*, remembered the enemy began shelling the town early on 26 May:

> *Geoff Gee moved the whole company into slit trenches by the colliery, which had been made by miners for ARP purposes. We were very close to a large slag heap* [this may have been the slag heap at Cité 1900] *which was being used as an observation post by French gunners. There were a lot of Jerry planes about ... a colliery building close to us had a direct hit; everyone was covered in brick and coal dust and, worse still, our two company trucks were buried under the debris of the building.*

Positioned north from the railway bridge at Pont-à-Vendin were A Company, some of whom faced the railway sidings and industrial complex of Vendin-le-Veil. Private Horace Greasley must have been further north along the canal, as he mentions a small stone bridge carrying a road between two farms on opposite banks of the canal. He and his comrades were asleep in the farm on the eastern bank when the German attack began. As Greasley and his platoon ran to take up their positions, German infantry was seen approaching the bridge which, according to Greasley, had still not been destroyed. Opening fire with the Bren gun and supported by a volley of rifle fire, the German attempts to cross the bridge were initially thwarted. But any congratulatory cheers were quickly dispelled by German infantry, who having crossed the canal through gaps in the defences, were now working their way behind the A Company positions. Outflanked and outgunned, Greasley's platoon was soon taken prisoner. Realizing the battalion was now in no position to continue the fight, Ruddle gave orders, to what men he could muster, to withdraw across country. Lance Corporal Mortimer-Jones, a battalion driver, was sheltering in a slit trench at Carvin when his truck was destroyed in a bombing raid with most of his personal kit. Retrieving a Boys rifle, which he carried all the way home to England, he found himself alone and facing the long walk to La Panne. Scrounging the occasional lift he eventually got aboard HMS *Halcyon* and arrived home on 29 May. Like Mortimer-Jones, Richard Everard also got home but recalled the confusion that inevitably engulfed Battalion HQ at Carvin:

German assault engineers crossing the La Bassée Canal with elements of the SS *Totenkopf* Division.

We moved from the slit trenches [at the colliery] *across the railway lines to Battalion HQ. There was confusion there. The company became divided, half with Geoff and me and the rest with Eric Capron and CSM Monty Burton. We received orders from the CO to withdraw across country. In this confusion and chaos I saw Lieutenant Charlie Hughes* [Transport Officer] *and Lieutenant Botibol* [Intelligence Officer], *and it was the last time I ever did see them. They were killed within the next few days.*

In hindsight it has to be said that once the 2/5 Leicesters began to dig in along the canal on 25 May their destruction was an inevitable finale. They stood little chance against a German division that barely paused as they crossed the canal. No official records exist of the battalion's movements after 26 May, although a party of some seventy men under Major Ken Symington were part of the Dunkerque rearguard, holding the Bergues Canal at Coudekerque until they were ordered to the beaches to be evacuated. Amongst those who got home was Ken Ruddle, who survived the campaign and retired in 1942. Not a young man when the battalion went to France, the campaign was the final straw in a long military career.

Chapter Six

6 Brigade at St-Venant and Robecq

Despite the Halt Order remaining in force until 3.30pm on Sunday 26 May, there were at least two enemy incursions on 24 May. Guderian, as we know, had sanctioned Sepp Dietrich's SS- *Leibstandarte* Adolf Hitler to cross the canal at Watten to take the high ground to the east, but whether Reinhardt knew of the SS-*Verfügungs* Division's incursion between Thiennes and Robecq is unclear. There is certainly a 'grey area' surrounding the orders for the *Verfügungs'* assault: were they issued before the Halt Order, or afterwards?

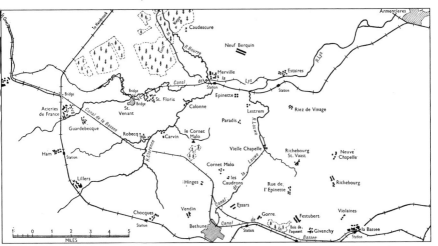

A map from *The Manchester Regiment Regular Battalions 1922-1948* showing the area of the Canal Line from Aire-sur-la-Lys to La Bassée.

The German advance on 24 May was spearheaded by three battalions of the SS-*Germania* Regiment, who were ordered across the canal at Robecq, Busnes and the road bridge at Guarbecque and to move on St-Venant, a small town that lay two miles north on the canalised River Lys. Having thrown temporary bridges over the canal, the 15/Motorcycle Company, commanded by *Hauptsturmführer* Mulhenkamp, set out for Robecq, whilst other detachments of the SS headed westwards towards St-Venant.

79

Men of the Germania Regiment. The soldier on the left has a range finder tripod over his left shoulder and is holding a Luger pistol.

The German advance certainly threw the West Yorkshires into disarray. HQ Company was pushed back towards Calonne, but B and C Companies were left isolated in position along the canal. It was a situation that was rapidly becoming untenable and, with German forces pouring into Robecq, B and C Companies were eventually forced to leave their canal side positions and retire towards Calonne-sur-la-Lys (Calonne).

Rustyforce

At 3.00am on 25 May, Polforce was dissolved and the next day responsibility for the defence of the Canal line south east of Busnes became the responsibility of Rustyforce, under the command of 50-year-old Major General Thomas Ralph Eastwood. This was yet another *ad hoc* collection of available troops, which on this occasion, went under the name of Eastwood's nickname, 'Rusty'. The 26 May was also the day on which two brigades of the 48th Division were dispatched to Cassel, Hazebrouck and Wormhout to hold the western edge of the so-called Dunkerque corridor. As the Manchester's Regimental historian remarked, the situation had become almost desperate:

Major General Ralph Eastwood, taken in 1938.

> *The word corridor is, in itself, a description of the peril to which the British Army then stood; for of all bad positions, a corridor that is being attacked on both sides is assuredly the worst.*

Thus, in reality, only the Canal Line east of Robecq through to Râches remained in British hands. The French First Army still held the line from Râches to the British sector on the Frontier Line. It was the French First Army that defended the southern aspect of the Dunkerque corridor at Lille for four days against seven German divisions between 28 and 31 May; their magnificent fighting defence was an essential piece of the evacuation jigsaw, without which the story may have been very different.

The loss of St-Venant and Robecq now became the focus for 6 Brigade and their orders were to clear the Germans out of St-Venant and Calonne, to press them back across the canal defending the line running from the l'Epinette road bridge to the Blackfriars Bridge on the D937. It is worth noting that the withdrawal of the SS-*Verfügungs* back to the canal on 24 May was not driven by the Halt Order, but by the offensive advance of the 1/Royal Welch Fusiliers. Their task was a tall order for any battalion to undertake; but for a severely under strength unit with little or no fire support, it was all but impossible.

The counter attack by the 1/Royal Welch Fusiliers

It was around 10.00am, shortly after the battalion had arrived at Vielle-Chapelle, that 43-year-old Lieutenant Colonel Herbert 'Harry' Harrison was summoned to Brigade HQ at Calonne and ordered to retake the four bridges near Robecq. On paper it looked relatively straightforward, but

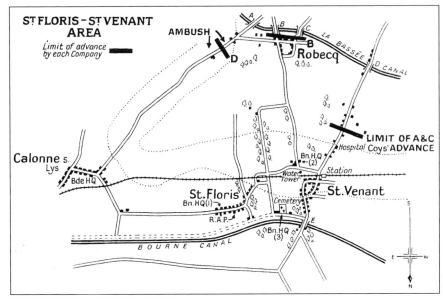

A map taken from *The Story of the Royal Welch Fusiliers 1919-1945*, depicting the counter attack, which began on 24 May, to retake the four bridges south of St-Venant.

in reality there were only four maps available to the whole battalion, forcing some company commanders to fight within the limit of their immediate vision of the battlefield. If that was not enough to contend with, the few remaining hours of daylight added to Harrison's concerns over the task in front of his battalion. Speed in this case was paramount and the battalion, led by Second Lieutenant John Garnett's Carrier Platoon, left at 6.00pm, contact with the enemy first being made on the eastern outskirts of St-Floris. As the two leading carriers forced their way through the village, German anti-tank guns knocked out both vehicles, killing the crews. John Garnett and six other fusiliers were killed; their graves are in the St-Floris churchyard cemetery. Pushing on in the fading daylight, the remainder of the Carrier Platoon neutralized the gun and the battalion secured the village perimeter. The Welch advance was stopped 'not by the lack of will to go forward, but by the hazard caused by darkness, lack of maps and unknown country'.

Lieutenant Robin Boyle, commanding D Company, who was in possession of one of the battalion's four maps, looked very much as if he had mistaken his orders. Rather than follow the battalion through St-Floris to Robecq, he took his company along the D69 – the direct route to Blackfriars Bridge [the name given to the bridge by troops during the First World War] down the Calonne – Robecq road. Leading the way was

16 Platoon with 17 and 18 Platoons checking the buildings on either side of the road for signs of the enemy. Just before Robecq the company was ambushed in the darkness and in the ensuing fire fight the 24-year-old Boyle was killed before the survivors managed to disengage and withdraw. The first shots had in fact set two hayricks alight on either side of the road, illuminating the whole company, and forcing them to take cover in the roadside ditches. Second Lieutenant Kemp, who assumed command of the company, quickly assessed the situation they found themselves in:

> *Under the prevailing conditions of bright illumination, wire obstacles and close hostile machine gun fire, he decided, in view of the growing casualty list, that it would be unwise to continue the attempt to work round the enemy's flanks. Since the company was doing no good where it was, he* [Kemp] *ordered a withdrawal.*

As darkness fell, Lieutenant Colonel Harrison had no clear idea of exactly where all his companies were and, without maps or information concerning the strength of enemy forces, any further attempts to reach the canal seemed inadvisable. Withdrawing his companies around St-Floris for the night, and establishing a temporary HQ on the western outskirts of the village, Harrison suspended operations until first light on 25 May.

Continuing the advance early the next morning, St-Venant was cleared by A and C Companies but they were subsequently held up just south of the hospital on the D916, where they dug in. Captain James Johnson and B Company fought their way into Robecq but heavy machine-gun fire prevented them from reaching the bridge. Intent on holding on to their positions, Johnson began fortifying the village, discovering too late that the enemy had worked round behind him and surrounded his company. Whether they expected to be relieved or not, there was little they could do that evening, apart from strengthening their defensive positions around the brewery at the intersection of the Calonne and St-Venant roads. Johnson was wounded later that evening and command devolved to Second Lieutenant Michael Edwards.

The 1/Royal Berkshires

Apparently unaware of the situation in which the Royal Welch had become embroiled, Brigadier Dennis Furlong, commanding 6 Brigade, ordered the 1/Royal Berkshires on 24 May to seize the bridges over the canal at Guarbecque to protect the western side of the corridor to Dunkerque, a task they were told would be relatively straightforward.

With the battalion split into two columns, one directed towards Guarbecque and the other to Haverskerque, Lieutenant Colonel Geoffrey Bull's suspicions that all was not as it appeared were first raised by an artillery barrage, which greeted his battalion's exit from St-Venant and then by heavy machine-gun fire as it advanced towards Guarbecque on the D186. The bridge over the Lys Canal had been partially destroyed and, after some hasty repairs under shellfire, C Company crossed over to Haverskerque. Without artillery support and unsure of the strength of enemy forces ahead of him, Bull sensibly withdrew the remainder of the battalion around le Bas Hamel to hold the long bend of the canal. Sadly he died of wounds received on 28 May after being evacuated to England. He is buried in Hammersmith Old Cemetery, London. On 27 May enemy attacks on Battalion HQ le Bas Hamel prompted a successful counter attack led by Major Horace Rew:

> *That restored the situation with the same tolerant nonchalance that attends manoeuvres when the august of a unit suffer indignities at the hands of an enterprising but slightly too exuberant enemy. The enemy attack finally subsided with the arrival of the reserve company and a discreet battalion withdrawal* [to Haverskerque], *under heavy fire, followed.*

The 2/Durham Light Infantry

Captain Cyril Townsend's diary for Saturday 25 May 1940 tells us that the 2/DLI left Calonne in companies and marched by separate routes to occupy the line of the railway that ran through St-Venant. Townsend was the Durham's adjutant and the commanding officer was Lieutenant Colonel Robert 'Bobby' Simpson, an officer who had been appointed to command the battalion in March 1940. Simpson, like many of his contemporaries, had served in the First World War, arriving in France as a fresh faced subaltern in December 1917. By the time the battalion arrived at St-Venant the surviving men of the Durhams were marching in four amalgamated companies, a situation that was not improved by the temporary loss of two companies a week earlier near Overyssche. The war diary does not record a further reorganization but it is likely there was some additional redistribution of

Captain Cyril Townsend kept a detailed diary of the Durhams in France and Flanders.

men on the mistaken assumption the two missing companies had been overwhelmed by the enemy.

The deployment at St-Venant

Meanwhile Lieutenant Colonel Harrison had established the Welch Fusiliers Headquarters near the railway station at St-Venant and, leaving Major Owen, the second in command to collect and redirect men to their new positions, he set off with his adjutant to establish contact with Lieutenant Colonel Simpson and the Durhams.

The former railway station at St-Venant was close to where Lieutenant Colonel Harrison established his headquarters before moving to the communal cemetery.

The Welch line ran along the road running south of the railway from the level crossing to the crossroads at the eastern end of the embankment and covered the bridge over the canal, where they were in touch with the Durhams. The Welch anti-aircraft machine guns were positioned in the small wood next to the cemetery and somewhere in the vicinity was the Manchester Regiment's machine gun platoon.

That still left the gap between the outskirts of St-Venant and the Berkshires. Simpson was obviously concerned about the vulnerability of the gap and deployed a combined B and D Company with Lieutenant John Gregson on the right flank and the remaining three companies along the railway line between the Robecq and Rue des Amuzoires. Establishing his Battalion Headquarters in the Taverne farmhouse near the canal, Simpson managed to place the battalion transport under cover in one of the barns. However, the left flank, like that on the right, appeared to be wide open, and it was this flank that would ultimately seal the fate of many of those at St-Venant. The brigade was supported by the ever faithful 44/Battery from 13/Anti-Tank Regiment and 226/Battery from 57/Anti-Tank Regiment, who had been detached from the 44th Division, together with the guns of 99 (Buckinghamshire Yeomanry) Field Regiment.

C Company, 2/Manchester Regiment
Still with 6 Brigade was Captain George Frampton and the machine guns of C Company, 2/Manchesters, that had fought with them on the Dyle and Escaut. The battalion was under the command of Lieutenant Colonel Edward 'Dick' Holmes but, as with almost every machine gun battalion, the companies were allocated to particular brigades and the regiment did not fight as a complete unit. Holmes, who managed to get back to England, surrendered to the Japanese at Singapore, along with the survivors of 2/Manchesters, in February 1942, in what was considered the largest surrender of British-led military personnel in history. Incredibly, he survived his captivity.

By nightfall on 25 May C Company were in St-Venant with their HQ on the southern edge of the Forêt de Nieppe. [Battalion HQ was at Richebourg.] Frampton reports that there was some difficulty in 'making a firm joining point between the Bois de Paqueant on 4 Brigade's right flank and the left flank of 6 Brigade' a gap that appears not to have been closed by nightfall. [The Bois du Pacault was the ideal cover for the resumption of the German attack.] When the end came at St-Venant, the surviving men of C Company fought on with the Durhams and Royal Welch Fusiliers. Frampton was one of only six officers from the Manchesters who made it home via Dunkerque.

99 (Buckinghamshire Yeomanry) Field Regiment
With the outbreak of war the regiment was mobilised at Aylesbury and in January 1940 they were sent to France as part of the 2nd Division with two batteries of twelve guns. The experience of the BEF in 1940 highlighted the problem with this organization: field regiments were intended to support an infantry brigade of three battalions, which could not be managed effectively with two batteries. As a result, field regiments were later reorganized into three batteries of eight guns. Lieutenant Colonel Francis Watson was in command of the regiment until 23 May, after which he assumed the temporary responsibilities of divisional CRA when Brigadier Findlay was reassigned to Finforce. Command was

devolved to 42-year-old Major John Whiteley, who appears from the war diary to have been in command of the regiment during the engagement at St-Venant. A First World War veteran and Conservative Party politician, Whiteley – who was a brigadier three years later – was killed along with General Wladyslaw Sikorski, the exiled leader of the Polish government, when the aircraft he was a passenger in crashed into the sea off Gibraltar in July 1943.

The regiment came into action on 25 May at Calonne and St-Floris. Late on 26 May the batteries were moved to a new position near Haverskerque and came into action again against the German advance the next morning. Major Anthony Clifton-Brown, commanding 394/ Battery was badly wounded during the action and by 10.00am the regiment's guns were in action defending Regimental Headquarters against German armour which had crossed the canal and headed north. The war diary, short as it is, gives a flavour of the fighting:

> *One 18-pounder from 393 Battery brought to RHQ as anti-tank. Tanks were engaged at 300 yards and two put out of action. Other tanks were knocked out during the day by both batteries. Throughout the day the work accomplished by armoured Observation posts was invaluable. The enemy got round both flanks and the group was finally compelled to withdraw.*

Robecq

As night fell on St-Venant, the surrounded Welshmen at Robecq could only listen to the movement of enemy forces crossing the canal and await the onslaught that would come the next morning. It began at 7.30am with a barrage of artillery and mortar fire which preceded the 1/IR 3 attack along the Eclème road. *Infanterist* Hofmann and his company were waiting to advance once the guns had ceased firing:

> *At 7.30am exactly our artillery began firing on Robecq. Houses burst into flames as they were hit; the grey skies above were traced with red light. However our artillery had little effect and nothing moved in the area; even after 300 rounds the nervous silence hung over the rooftops ... We approached the village, our commander leading the way. We had just passed the first houses and we still had not heard a single shot. The road seemed deserted and with each step we took the silence seemed to deepen. The crossroads loomed in front of us; there was the cemetery. It was at this moment that a heavy weight of fire rained down from the surrounding houses.*

The memorial at Robecq.

Slowly B Company were driven back into a continually contracting perimeter but with flat ground all around there was little chance of a break-out succeeding in daylight. Edwards split the remaining men of the company into small groups and ordered them to attempt to get back under cover of darkness. But it was not to be. The regimental historian concludes his description of B Company's stand with the words 'At 11.00am B Company ceased to exist'. Edwards was taken prisoner along with the majority of the survivors, while Johnson, with a bullet wound in the neck and back, was taken to the former English hospital at Camiers, from where he eventually made a successful escape over the Pyrenees to Spain.

The German assault on St-Venant

Quite why Brigadier Furlong deployed 6 Brigade south of the Lys Canal at St-Venant is puzzling, but it proved to be an error, contributing significantly to the destruction of the two defending the crossing. It was a decision made even more questionable by his refusal to grant Harrison's appeal to withdraw north of the canal on 26 May, a request that was also made by Lieutenant Colonel Simpson:

> *who forcibly pointed out to the Brigadier the danger that was developing from the left flank and had advocated withdrawing part of the battalion north of the St-Venant Canal.*

Furlong's award of the DSO for his command of 6 Brigade specifically mentions the 48 hours of the St-Venant defence, 'not withstanding the very heavy casualties they suffered'. He was killed on the Yorkshire coast on 5 September 1940 whilst inspecting a mine field. It is said that very few of the surviving officers and men from 6 Brigade who fought at St-Venant mourned his passing.

The German assault on 6 Brigade began at around 7.00am on 27 May under the overall command of *Oberst* Ulrich Kleemann, who moved across the La Bassée Canal with three battalions of infantry, a battery of guns from FAR 75 and elements of the *SS-Germania* Regiment. Kleemann's infantry assault was announced by a heavy artillery bombardment which, noted a delighted Second Lieutenant Michael Farr, did not prevent the combined fire of the Welch and Durham riflemen mowing [them] 'down like ninepins'. Farr's diary account of his service with the DLI lends a fresh aspect to the fighting, although on this occasion his euphoria was short-lived: the heavy growl of tanks could be heard behind the infantry, swaying the battle in the Germans' favour. It was the beginning of the end. Cyril Townsend's diary again:

Oberst **Ulrich Kleemann was in command of the attack on St-Venant on 27 May.**

Heavy mortar fire and possibly artillery fire was put down on our company positions. The church spire was hit and movement in the village was difficult and dangerous. The enemy was moving across our front to the left. About 15 tanks could be seen from battalion HQ. Our artillery opened fire but later ceased firing.

The combined B and D Company – with its headquarters at the junction of the Rue de Hurtevent and Rue d'Aire – was on the western edge of St-Venant, with the Guarbecque stream to their front. Having been joined by Sergeant Martin McLane and some of his men from the Mortar Platoon, they were on the extreme right flank of the battalion with no contact between themselves and the Royal Berkshires. The previous day enemy artillery fire had claimed the life of 24-year-old Lieutenant John Gregson, who was hit with 'a bowl-sized piece of shrapnel' which lodged in the base of his spine, leaving command of the company to CSM Norman Metcalf.

Sergeant Martin McLane.

The events of 27 May on the B and D Company front are largely confined to those few accounts that have survived the ravages of time. Once the tanks moved in the company was heavily engaged but without heavy weapons their struggle against armoured vehicles became futile. Inevitably, as their resistance collapsed, the fighting became fractured, with small groups of men defending their own piece of ground. Private Dusty Miller who, with his mate, George Blackburn, was in front of a privet hedge near a farm: 'we could hear shots going through the hedge, like the sound of bees; we were pinned down and couldn't do anything'.

Back in St-Venant the story was much the same. The Royal Welch lost heavily as their much depleted companies came up against enemy armour. A Company, which had already been reduced to two platoons, was soon overwhelmed after being completely surrounded. Twenty-nine-year-old Captain Edward Parker-Jervis, commanding C Company, was killed defending a house, which had been surrounded, and D Company, under Second Lieutenant Kemp, could only muster fifteen men after they retired towards the canal in the face of several German tanks, with a wounded PSM Jenkins being pushed along in a wheelbarrow. Nevertheless, with 6 Brigade contesting every inch of ground, enemy units were finding the British defence hard to overcome. Men of 8 *Kompanie* II/IR 3 found the advance up the Busnes road to be painfully slow as they moved from house to house, losing *Leutnant* Wallenburg as they reached the railway line. Also taking heavy casualties was 7

The hospital at St-Venant where *Major* Zimmermann of II/IR 3 established his battalion's HQ.

Kompanie, which reached the water tower by the station under a hail of fire:

> *Leutnant von Bismark was fatally wounded in this attempt. He was quickly taken to a field hospital but was dead on arrival. The company engaged the enemy in the town and a street battle raged, fought across the ruins and debris of burning houses ... During this time Major Zimmermann set up his battalion HQ in the hospital and 6 Kompanie managed to reach the town; in so doing they suffered casualties at the hands of a few isolated machine gunners.*

Forced back onto the Lys Canal, a runner arrived at Simpson's DLI headquarters at Taverne's Farm with a message from Lieutenant Colonel Harrison, who had by this time moved his Royal Welch HQ to the northern end of the communal cemetery. Cyril Townsend, not knowing exactly where his commanding officer was, made the perilous journey

A photograph of the Canal Bridge at St-Venant taken in 1918 during the German Lys offensive. The 18-pounder is pointing to the south and the estaminet, which can be seen on the far bank of the canal, may well be the one highlighted by Captain Cyril Townsend.

along the canal bank where Harrison told him of his intention to hold the canal bridge to enable the survivors to get across:

> *I crawled back to see Colonel Harrison. He said the position was untenable and that he was taking what men he could to form a bridgehead. I was to bring back any men I could. I sent Lyster-Todd and some men back at once and crawled forward to find CSM Birkitt and Private Worthy, the C Company runner. By this time armoured cars had almost reached the café and although I waved to the men inside, I realized they could no more come out than I could go to them across open space.*

The bridge over the canal was the only exit available. It had been destroyed by the retreating Germans on 24 May and replaced by the Royal Engineers when St-Venant was recaptured. But for Simpson and the men at the Durhams' headquarters, it now became a bridge too far as German armour closed in, some of which may have advanced from the right flank after disposing of the DLI defence on Rue d'Aire. Harrison's move to the canal crossing was in response to Brigadier Furlong's orders to retire, but there is some discussion as to what time Furlong actually arrived. The account in *Y Ddraig Gogh* says 9.15am, Townsend's diary declared Furlong arrived at 11.00am with orders for the brigade to retire, but Michael Farr was

Lieutenant Michael Farr.

quite sure that no orders for retirement arrived at the Durhams' headquarters at Taverne's Farm. He may of course have been too occupied with the severity of the fighting to notice the arrival of anything other than German armour:

> *I saw the position getting more and more serious. The Boche had infiltrated around the left flank, snipers had crossed the canal and the bastards were shooting our soldiers in the back. Meanwhile huge and ugly tanks were bearing down upon us. Our one and only anti-tank gun was destroyed. The men were driven to the edge of the river bank; they had nowhere to go but backwards into the water.*

The Durhams' last stand by the canal was made at the barn, which by now was under fire and in flames, with Simpson defiantly firing his pistol at German tanks which were advancing up the Rue des Amusoires. Enemy units had also got in behind them after advancing along the undefended left flank. Surrounded and almost out of ammunition, the Durhams had little choice but to throw down their weapons and surrender.

After Cyril Townsend had left Harrison's Headquarters, Captain Walter Clough-Taylor was instructed by Harrison to form a defensive flank by the bridge, but first they had to run the gauntlet of enemy fire to get there:

> I saw many men stagger and fall as they ran. Martin, my trusty servant, had his arm blown off. Then it was my turn. I summoned courage, waited for a burst of fire and dashed forward. I was only a yard or so on to the bridge when I was hit in the leg, I recoiled and staggered crazily back to the culvert. As I stood thinking wildly how I was going to get across alive, I noticed there were girders rising to about a foot in height in the centre, above the roadway ... I got up and was at once hit again in the arm and hip, I staggered on to the shelter of some houses.

Clough-Taylor was taken prisoner but a few of the Durhams did manage to get across the bridge with Townsend, who was shot through the face as he reached the other side. He remembered a Welshman putting a field dressing on the wound before he managed to walk away under more machine-gun fire. He describes the final moments at the bridge:

> When Colonel Harrison saw that no one else could get across the bridge owing to the close proximity of the leading tanks, which by this time were only 150 yards away, he ordered the Royal Engineers to blow [it]; unfortunately there were none available. The situation then became impossible as there were perhaps twenty men holding the bridge with only one Bren gun and no anti-tank rifle against at least five tanks. The leading tank came across the bridge and wiped out most of the men holding it.

The leading German tank hesitated before crossing the bridge and bringing its fire to bear on the cottages ahead. Harrison was killed 'in the last flurry of fighting while attempting to delay the crossing' and those that could began making their way north towards le Touquet where 6 Brigade Headquarters was situated. As a battalion the RWF were

93

effectively wiped out, losing 759 men, with only three officers and eighty men making it to Dunkerque.

On the right flank the surviving men of the DLI were also heading for the Lys Canal. Dusty Miller remembers there were tanks approaching when he heard the order from Martin McLane to make for the canal:

We started running across a field, I did not know there was a canal there, I don't think any of the other lads knew there was a canal ... As we were running, George was behind me and I heard him shout 'Jim, Jim', so I stopped and George was lying on his back, he had been hit in the legs I think, I ran back towards him and I saw a young officer running towards me and he shouted 'keep going, keep going' and I had to leave George.

Fortunately George survived to be taken prisoner and Dusty Miller was taken prisoner in the Forest of Nieppe. The young officer may well have been Second Lieutenant Jasper Rudd who, with some sixty men, made his way through the Forest of Nieppe to find the B Echelon transport. Rudd was a territorial officer who had been transferred from 9/DLI; he left the battalion in 1941 to join the Royal Engineers. The remnants of the carrier platoon, consisting of about fifteen men and three carriers, held a position against a number of tanks in front of le Touquet, northeast of Haverskerque, where Brigade HQ was situated, until they was ordered to retire through the Forest of Nieppe. The carrier platoon acted as rearguard to the remaining part of the brigade, which consisted largely of Royal Berkshires.

The sacrifice of the two 6 Brigade battalions at St-Venant was an almost inevitable conclusion from the moment they took up position along the railway line. The Berkshires, although attacked at dawn on 27 May, did manage 'a discreet battalion withdrawal, under heavy fire' to new positions behind the Lys Canal; but there are still over twenty identified men buried locally. That evening only 212 officers and men of the Berkshires answered their names at roll call. The casualty list for the St-Venant defenders was significantly greater, as the CWGC cemeteries in the area bear witness. In the St-Venant Communal Cemetery there are over 120 identified men who were killed in the action, including Captain Edward Parker-Jervis. Lieutenant Colonel Harrison and a further five of his men lie in the Haverskerque British Cemetery, while the Robecq Communal Cemetery contains the Fusiliers of B and D Company. This number does not take into account the unidentified dead – whose names appear on the Dunkirk Memorial – the wounded and those taken prisoner.

Yet there is a darker side to the casualty lists that first came to light

After the battle. Durham Light Infantry prisoners outside the church at St-Venant.

when the dead at St-Venant were reinterred from the mass grave they had originally been buried in. Post mortem files indicated that in a number of cases there were impact blows to the skull, which could only have been inflicted at close range. The testimony from the local population and from survivors point to units of the *SS-Germania* Regiment being responsible for the shooting and bayoneting of British prisoners to the west of the town after they had surrendered. In the subsequent inquiry, the Judge Advocate's Office initially found that six prisoners had been executed in this manner and although the perpetrators were identified as SS soldiers from the *Germania* Regiment, their names remain unknown. In addition there is also a body of evidence that suggests other war crimes against wounded and captured British soldiers in the vicinity did take place, although to date no confirmation has surfaced in the public domain. There may still be MI 19 documents which are still classified and unavailable for public scrutiny and until these files – if they exist – are examined, the full story of the St-Venant murders will remain untold.

Chapter Seven

4 Brigade and the Paradis Massacre

The brigade was under the command of 47-year-old Brigadier Edward Warren who, up until February 1940, had commanded the 2/Northamptons. Along with the 1/8 Lancashire Fusiliers and the 2/Royal Norfolks, the 1/Royal Scots were withdrawn from the Escaut at midnight on 22 May and ordered to the La Bassée Canal, which was to become the graveyard of so many of the officers and men of the 2nd Division. Of the ninety officers and 2,480 other ranks of 4 Brigade, which had advanced into Belgium on 10 May, only twenty-five officers and 697 other ranks mustered on 15 June to reform the brigade. A single stark sentence in the brigade war diary recorded that, 'no commanding officer, 2nd in Command, Adjutant, nor any forward Company Commander of the three battalions appeared from amongst the stragglers.'

'A' Field Regiment, Royal Artillery
On 17 May Lieutenant Colonel Edward Burns, commanding the Royal Artillery Instruction Wing, was ordered to put together a regiment of 18-pounders and support the 23rd Division, a formation he later found out had been almost annihilated near Arras. In the event he was only able to find eighteen assorted guns before he was ordered to Béthune, where he came under the orders of 46th Division and then, finally, the 2nd Division. The regiment only existed for a fortnight and was divided into five batteries, which were deployed along the canal covering the crossing points in the same manner as 392/Battery had done between St-Momelin and Wittes. Burns was not a man to mince his words and the war diary, short as it is, does give a flavour of the man who commanded, what the CRE of the 2nd Division called, Burns's Tigers.

Regiment completely untrained; unarmed; and had never been together in any capacity. Found no telephones, radio transmitters, instruments or the means of getting it into action as a field regiment, so deployed it up close as an anti-tank unit instead. No Medical arrangements. An artillery nightmare; but can fight over open sights or through the bore if no sights. Heavy air fighting, but no casualties. French in retreat from 1st and 9th French Armies.

*Scenes of wildest confusion and extreme cowardice in French
Armies.*

Burns does mention in the war diary that Major Cubitt's 392/Battery was
attached to his regiment; but it would appear that either this did not
actually take place or, if it did, was a momentary attachment that was
dissolved when Burns was ordered to the Béthune area. This was in the
area defended initially by the 1/RIF and then by 4 Brigade. During the
battle eight of Burns' guns were completely destroyed, two detachments
were killed or badly wounded and six more guns were either lost or
destroyed. In what Sir Martin Farndale calls 'The Battle of the Bridges'
Burns' unit certainly 'prevented disaster and the gallantry of its men were
in the highest traditions of the regiment'.

2/Royal Norfolk Regiment

The Norfolks were now under the command of their third
commanding officer, 37-year-old Major Lisle Ryder, who
had taken charge after his predecessor had been wounded
on the Escaut. Lisle Ryder was the brother of Robert
Dudley Ryder who, as a Commander RN, led the raid on
St-Nazaire in 1942, resulting in his award of the Victoria
Cross. Even before the battalion arrived on the canal to take
up their allotted sector between the Bois du Pacault and the
bridge at Béthune, two companies of Norfolks had
inadvertently deployed to a subsidiary loop in the canal,
leaving a large gap on the left flank and no doubt increasing
Ryder's unease. Although the wayward companies were

**Robert Dudley
Ryder VC.**

back in place twenty-four hours later, the Pioneer Section from HQ
Company had been pushed into the gap by Ryder and told to make every
round count. Private Ernie Farrow and his mates found that by using rifle
fire instead of the more 'ammunition hungry' Bren gun they were able to
conserve on ammunition and bluff the Germans into thinking 'there was
a great company of us there'. To Farrow's amazement they managed to
hold off the German assault until B and D Companies finally turned up.

That evening Ryder withdrew his headquarters to Duries Farm on the
Chemin de Paradis, about 500 yards west of the Paradis crossroads, where
Farrow and the surviving pioneers rejoined. The scene that confronted
him was shocking:

*I ran into this cow shed and was amazed to see all my comrades
lying about, some of them had lost a foot, some an arm, they were
laying about everywhere, being tended by the bandsmen who were*

Looking towards Béthune, the picture shows transport from the 7ᵗʰ Panzer Division crossing the canal.

all first aid men. The first thing I wanted was a cigarette, I wanted a fag. I was dying! I'd never smoked a lot but this time to save my nerves I found someone who had some fags, and I just smoked my head off.

Overnight on 26 May, German forces, including the SS-*Totenkopf* Division, moved up the south bank of the La Bassée Canal in preparation for an assault on British forces the next morning. Temporary pontoon bridges were quickly put across the water to enable armoured vehicles to cross. Advancing with the 2ⁿᵈ Battalion, *SS-Totenkopf* Division, was Herbert Brunnegger and 3 *Kompanie,* who crossed the ruins of the bridge at Pont Supplie on the D184, where he came across his first wounded British soldier:

His face is distinctive and brown but the proximity of death is making his skin go pale. He is standing up and leaning against a wall made of earth. In his eyes there is an indescribably hopeless expression while the whole time bright spurts of blood are coming out of a wound at the base of his neck. In vain his hands try to press on a vein in order to try and keep the life in his body. He cannot be saved.

The fierce fighting around le Cornet Malo – which was held by the Norfolks – slowed the SS advance considerably, although Private Arthur Brough, who was with the B Company Mortar Platoon, considered it was getting a bit hectic:

Lots of tanks and heavy gunfire. We were putting as much stuff down the mortar as we could. We were trying to repulse them but we knew it wasn't a lot of good because there were so many there ... The mortar must have been red hot, anything we could get hold of we were putting down the mortar until it got so bad that we even resorted to rifles.

There were only three of the platoon left standing when Brough and his mates resorted to firing their rifles at the approaching enemy, which they continued to do until the arrival of enemy tanks, at which point he confesses they 'just ran for it'.

A rather grainy photograph of men of the 4th Panzer Division carrying a badly wounded comrade back across the canal.

The actual detail of the fighting remains obscure but we do know from the various war diaries that with the aid of several counter-attacks and with assistance from the Royal Scots, a fragile equilibrium was restored by nightfall, with the Germans in occupation of Riez du Vinage and the

Bois du Pacault. But there had been heavy casualties on both sides and only about sixty men of A and B Companies of the Norfolks remained capable of fighting, leaving Lieutenant Murray-Brown wondering just how long they would be able to 'hold the position to the last man and the last round'. It was, he thought, getting a little desperate.

The attack continued at 3.00am the next morning with German forces emerging from the shelter of the Bois Pacault. Brunnegger and his *Kompanie* moved slowly towards le Cornet Malo:

> *The attack is renewed. A weak sun is rising out of the ground mist. A signpost points to Le Cornet Malo. Mortars and sub-machine guns move into position on the edge of the wood and fire at recognizable targets in a village a couple of hundred metres in front of us. While they do this our soldiers move forward on both sides of the path ... Onwards! A surprise as bursts of machine-gun fire hit a section as it moves out of a cutting. The bursts toss them into a tangle of bodies. One stands up and sways past me to the rear – he has a finger stuck into a hole in his stomach.*

If Brunnegger thought for a moment that the fight for le Cornet Malo would be relatively easy, his confidence was to be rudely shattered by the dogged defence of the Norfolks and the Royal Scots:

> *The English defend themselves with incredible bravery ... we are completely pinned to the ground in front of the enemy who are totally invisible and whose ability commands our admiration. We have to adapt ourselves completely to the enemy's tactics. We work ourselves forward by creeping, crawling and slithering along. The enemy retreat skilfully without showing themselves.*

However, overwhelmed by the sheer number of German soldiers and their supporting artillery, and with the village in flames, the survivors were slowly pushed back on Paradis.

1/Royal Scots

A Company of the Royal Scots, having now moved east, was in position three quarters of a mile south east of le Cornet Malo, astride the present day D945 Merville road, when they beat off a strong German force heading north from the canal. During the fighting Major Butcher was badly wounded but continued to be carried around on the broad back of CSM Johnstone until the arrival of Harold Money, who sent him up to the Regimental Aid Post (RAP) in Paradis. In the subsequent fighting both of the remaining subalterns were either killed or captured, leaving Johnstone to maintain their hold on the farm buildings they had by now fortified:

> *The Jocks did their best to turn the place into a strongpoint, blocking windows with tables and chairs and piling grain bags filled with earth in the gateway. Here they were prepared to make a last stand. Everyone realized that there must be no relinquishing a position from which they could deny the enemy passage up this important road.*

The Scots' headquarters at Paradis was in a farm complex on the Rue de Derrière with the RAP nearby, along the same road, closer to the village, was Major Watson's D Company Headquarters. Realizing a strong attack up the Merville road was forthcoming, Money pulled the remains of Captain Mackinnon and B Company – which up until this point, had been deployed along the Rue de Cerisiers – back into the village. Further south, A Company had beaten off several enemy attacks before Captain Nick Hallett of the Norfolks arrived from the direction of le Cornet Malo and ordered Johnstone to withdraw. But it was too late. Caught trying to escape along a ditch, the surviving men surrendered and Johnstone – accused of 'gouging out the eyes of dead German soldiers with his jack-knife' – was led into a field along with his companions to be shot. 'By a piece of good luck a staff officer in this division happened to come along in a car. He spoke to me in English and it was he who saved us from being shot.'

The picture shows a captured French Soma-35 that has been brought into service with the SS-*Totenkopf* Division. The picture was taken near le Cornet Malo on 27 May.

At Paradis, Harold Money was wounded and sent off to the La Gorge dressing station, which was the very spot he had been taken to in May 1915 after he had been wounded in the First World War. The end of the battalion's stand arrived with a ferocious German attack that shattered the buildings of the village. Lance Corporal James Howe was in the Royal Scots' RAP at Paradis when SS troops first appeared:

> We were with the Royal Norfolks; they had one end of the village and we had the other ... We were about fifty yards from the centre of the village. We were in this house tending our wounded in the RAP, with the medical officer and the padre with about six of us attendants, and maybe twenty wounded ... the first thing I saw was a hand preparing to throw a hand grenade through the window of our aid post. This hand grenade came in, blew up and we all dived into the corner. Of course the building caught fire so we had no option but to get out as quickly as we could.

In a horrifying episode witnessed by Howe, a German NCO announced his intention to shoot the wounded Scots. Challenged by Padre MacLean and the Medical Officer, the NCO attempted to justify himself by saying the British had been using dum-dum bullets. It was only the intervention of those present that prevented the murder of wounded men. Whether or not any of the remaining Royal Scots were executed after they had surrendered is still open to conjecture, but there are reports in the various Paradis War Crimes files of men with similar wounds to the back of their heads being discovered in mass graves and another, which relates to evidence from a local Frenchwoman, of the apparent execution of seventeen Royal Scots found hiding in a hayloft. We will probably never know the truth of exactly what occurred on that afternoon in May 1940.

The Royal Scots' D Company made their last stand at a farm north of Paradis, where Major Watson was killed and James Bruce – now in command – held out long enough to allow him and a handful of men to escape. Sadly, they were captured near the Merville airfield 24 hours later. The dead of the Paradis massacre were exhumed from their mass grave in 1942 and moved to Le Paradis War Cemetery, where they now lie with the other casualties from 4 Brigade who were killed in that desperate engagement. Only five officers and ninety men of the Royal Scots eventually arrived home via Dunkerque.

D Company, 2/Manchester Regiment
The company was commanded by Captain Jack Churchill, an officer who would later go on to command the Commando Brigade in Italy. After

establishing his headquarters in a farm near le Bout de l'Epinette, Churchill was asked by Lieutenant Colonel Money to transport the Royal Scot's C Company from Calonne to a new position north of Bois du Pacault. En-route, Churchill remarks that he his men ran into a German patrol armed with automatic weapons. To the obvious surprise of the Germans, and the delight of Jack Churchill, the Royal Scots quickly debussed and killed or captured most of the patrol. Earlier, Churchill had been wounded in the ear by a burst of fire which

Captain Jack Churchill, taken later in the war.

shattered the windscreen of the truck he was travelling in; both he and his driver, Private Isles, were forced to jump clear and take temporary refuge in the roadside ditch. On 26 May Churchill moved 15 Platoon, with Lieutenants Chandler and Salt, to Riez du Vinage to enable them to fire on the western and northern edges of Bois du Pacault. At the same time 13 and 14 Platoons were moved to new positions on the road between Paradis and les Caudrons on the D182. [13 Platoon was initially deployed with the Royal Scots and 14 Platoon with the Norfolks.] The last stand of 13 Platoon was recorded by Sergeant Graves:

The following day a message was received from Brigade for 13 Platoon to proceed immediately to assist C Company of the Norfolk Regiment; 13 Platoon proceeded at once to this area and immediately went into action and successfully neutralized some forward slopes and positions the Jerries were preparing. The heavy and constant fire from 13 Platoon made the Jerry retire, enabling the remnants of the Norfolk company to drop back to some decent cover. To my surprise, all the infantry company consisted of was a 2nd Lieutenant and about eighteen or twenty men and no more ... Throughout the day of the 26th the enemy never approached on our front, but having seen enemy movements on the distant flanks and hearing the constant fire of 14 and 15 Platoons, I realized we were in danger of being cut off ... Our position was now getting critical and after consultation with Sergeant Smith, [James Smith, commanding the platoon] *we decided out only chance of still remaining an effective force was to retire about 600 yards to where some small slopes and woods offered us some cover, with at least some chance of pulling out when necessary. We approached the 2nd Lieutenant of the Norfolks*

and tried to explain, but he flatly refused to permit us to retire ...
The enemy was now attacking from all directions, except the rear,
and after holding them at bay, the 2nd Lieutenant decided our only
chance was a quick withdrawal, but having no transport and 400
yards of open country in the rear, it was too late.

The second lieutenant was more than likely William Willison, who is
commemorated with Sergeant James Smith on the Dunkirk Memorial.
Only four of the Manchesters survived the assault and were taken prisoner
along with Sergeant Graves. It was the same story everywhere, many of
the Manchester's gunners were killed while still firing, while others,
badly wounded like Lance Corporal Flude of 15 Platoon, were taken
prisoner and survived. Captain Churchill by this time was further north,
the Brigade war diary describing what took place:

All this time, at a strongpoint at Epinette, a section of Captain
Churchill's machine guns, two guns of Captain Strachan's anti-
tank company, and a platoon of the 1/8 Lancashire Fusiliers, with
the remnants of Brigade Headquarters, were closely embroiled.
They fought throughout the day and, thanks to Captain Churchill's
leadership, successfully managed to leave their positions and
cross the Lys at 10.30pm.

The Massacre at Louis Creton's Farm
At Duries Farm the perimeter defences were slowly being taken out by
enemy machine-gun sections. Signaller Robert Brown was in the
farmhouse when Major Ryder gave the men the option of surrendering
or trying to escape. By sheer luck Brown and two others made the
decision to leave the building by a door leading onto the road:

The smoke from the burning house was going that way so we
thought we'd keep in the smoke as extra cover in the hopes of
getting away. We went in a ditch at the side of the road and in the
ditch was the adjutant [Captain Charles Long], lying on the
ground wounded and the medical officer was there. We attempted
to go out of the ditch and cross the road but as we did so the
German patrols were coming up from the village of Paradis and
we couldn't get over.

Duries Farm represented the approximate boundary between the Norfolks
and the Royal Scots and the location of the farm on Chemin du Paradis

goes some way to explaining the tragic events that followed Ryder's surrender of HQ Company. The farm and its outbuildings was attacked by Brunnegger's battalion and Brown's decision to leave the farmhouse by the door facing the road undoubtedly saved his life, as he was taken prisoner by another unit moving up from the village. Ryder and the remaining men left through the stable door leading to the fields at the rear of the farm. Their fate was now in the hands of *Hauptsturmführer* Fritz Knoechlein's men. What happened next, as Ryder and the men of Headquarters Company were marched up the road to Louis Creton's farm, will always rank as one of the most appalling atrocities committed during the 1940 campaign in France. Signaller Albert Pooley was one of the men who had surrendered with Ryder:

Hauptsturmführer Fritz Knoechlein pictured with men of his company.

There were a hundred of us prisoners marching in column of threes. We turned off the dusty French road through a gateway and into a meadow beside the buildings of a farm. I saw, with one of the nastiest feelings I've ever had in my life, two heavy machine guns inside the meadow. They were manned and pointing at the head of our column.

Herbert Brunnegger was at the farm when he saw the column of prisoners by the barn:

Many of them reach out in despair towards me with pictures of their families ... As I look more closely I notice two heavy machine guns which have been set up in front of them. Whilst I look on, surprised that two valuable machine guns should be used to guard prisoners, a dreadful thought occurs to me. I turn to the nearest machinegun post and ask what is going on here. 'They are to be shot!' is the embarrassed answer.

105

Louis Creton, pictured in 1946 repairing the wall of the barn where the Norfolks were massacred.

Brunnegger's account goes on to say that he understood the orders for the prisoners to be shot had been given by Knoechlein. It is difficult to say exactly what we would do in Brunnegger's place, but he writes that he chose to leave the scene in order not to witness the murder of prisoners. It is highly probable that he must have heard the cries of the Norfolks as they were cut down by the barn wall. Albert Pooley wrote afterwards that he felt an icy hand grip his stomach as the guns opened fire on them:

> *For a few seconds the cries and shrieks of our stricken men drowned the crackling of the guns. Men fell like grass before a scythe. The invisible blade came nearer and then swept through me. I felt a searing pain in my left leg and wrist and pitched forward in a red world of tearing agony ... but even as I fell forward into a heap of dying men the thought stabbed my brain, 'If I ever get out of here the swine who did this will pay for it.'*

Pooley did have his revenge and Knoechlein was brought to trial in 1948 where his defence claimed the British had used soft-nosed dum-dum bullets and had misused a white flag of truce, all of which were denied by the prosecution team. But some of the most damming evidence was given by Albert Pooley and the other survivor of the massacre, William O'Callaghan, all of which resulted in Knoechlein's conviction and sentencing to death by hanging – which was carried out in January 1949.

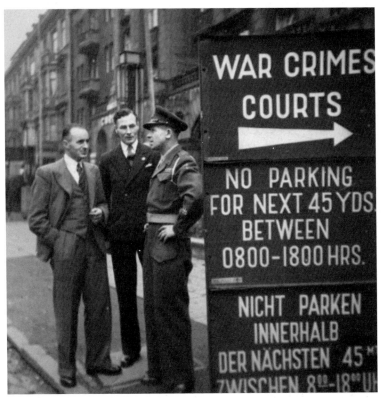

Albert Pooley (centre) and William O'Callaghan outside the Nuremberg Law
Courts during the trial of Fritz Knoechlein.

As for Albert Pooley's comrades, only three officers and sixty-nine other
ranks answered their names at the first roll call after Dunkerque.

The 1/8 Lancashire Fusiliers

Initially held in reserve at Epinette, the battalion was under the command
of a former 2/Dorset officer, Lieutenant Colonel David Stayner. Stayner
took over from Lieutenant Colonel Bird on 14 May while the battalion
was on the River Dyle in Belgium. After his capture on the canal the tall,
white haired Stayner eventually ended his wartime career in Colditz
Castle, where he became the senior British officer. On 25 May the
battalion was ordered to relieve the 1/Royal Irish Fusiliers on the canal
and Stayner took over Lieutenant Colonel Guy Gough's headquarters on
Rue Glattignies. Brigadier Warren must have known he was putting the
Lancashire men into what Gough called 'a very sticky proposition'.

Managing to withdraw under fire on 26 May, the Irish left a depleted battalion of Lancashire Fusiliers defending an increasingly precarious sector of the canal:

In the late evening, all units were warned that a large scale enemy attack was to be expected the following morning and the brigade would stand and fight. Only an hour after the receipt of this order, the enemy succeeded in making a penetration in the centre of the 1/8 Battalion's positions; though later the commanding officer was able to tell brigade that the battalion was holding its own and was still in position.

Lieutenant Colonel David Stayner, pictured at Colditz in 1941, with other senior Allied officers.

It was the heaviest attack the Fusiliers had yet encountered and before long communication with Battalion Headquarters had been cut, leaving isolated groups to fight their own battle amidst the increasing confusion of battle. Later that afternoon Warren gave the order to withdraw, but it was far too late, the battalion was surrounded and the surviving officers and men had little choice but to fight on until they were killed or captured. Apart from the war diary, there is no official account of what took place after the enemy crossed the canal, but there is a report written by the battalion medical officer, Lieutenant William Sillar, which throws some light onto the final hours of the garrison at Battalion Headquarters.:

Sometime in the afternoon [27 May] two German tanks were observed near the house at the corner of the farm road, and shortly thereafter others were observed approaching Battalion HQ across the field. At this point the regimental aid post was set on fire and became untenable ... Battalion HQ was now surrounded by four or more tanks, they circled around the farm within ten or twenty yards and, even at that range, our anti-tank rifles seemed to be quite ineffective. Men positioned outside the building were quickly put out of action ... The farmhouse was on fire and it was obvious that we were to be wiped out. The Colonel decided to surrender and walked out, followed by the dejected remainder – about twenty men.

A contemporary photograph of Gorre British and Indian Cemetery as British troops would have seen it in May 1940.

It is more than likely that one group of the 1/8 Lancashire Fusiliers did attempt to hold out in the Gorre British and Indian Cemetery, where many of the 55th (West Lancashire) Division are buried, casualties of the German offensive of April 1918. In the early days of the German occupation, Albert Roberts, who worked as a head gardener for the Imperial War Graves Commission, wrote that he kept on working as though nothing had happened:

> *I immediately visited all the cemeteries and memorial in my care.*
> *A great deal of damage had been done in the Gorre British and*
> *Indian Cemetery. Our troops had held position in the cemetery,*
> *dug trenches in many parts. I set about trying to clear debris and*
> *was able to later scythe the grass and clear up things in general.*
> *The surrounding wall was blown up over nearly its whole length,*
> *a large portion of headstones were smashed to pieces, the tool*
> *house had a direct hit.*

The battalion had, to all intents and purposes, ceased to exist. Apart from the five officers evacuated as wounded, only four officers and two hundred other ranks managed to return home. Fortunately, William Sillar was able to escape from captivity and return home via the Pyrenees. His MC was gazetted in 1941.

Captain William Sillar RAMC, photographed in 1943 after his escape.

109

Chapter Eight

5 Brigade and Festubert

The brigade was under the command of Brigadier Gerald Gartlan, a former officer of the 1/Royal Irish Rifles, who was no stranger to the flat country around the canal. In 1915 he took part in the Battle of Neuve Chapelle and four months later found himself embroiled in the Battles of Aubers Ridge and Fromelles. The officers and men of 5 Brigade suffered terribly during their defence of the canal, to the extent that, on 28 May 1940, there were only approximately twenty seven officers and 600 other ranks capable of answering their names.

2/Dorsetshire Regiment

There is an inconsistency between the 1/8 Lancashire Fusiliers war diary and the account written by the Dorset's historian, in that the positions occupied by the two battalions at Gorre do not match the evidence provided by John Horsfall and the Royal Irish Fusiliers. According to the account in the *History of the Devonshire Regiment*, the 2/Dorsets took over the canal line early on 25 May and B Company took over the positions in Gorre. However, Lieutenant John Horsfall, commanding D Company, 1/RIR, who was in Gorre village at the time, is adamant that the 1/8 Lancashire Fusiliers arrived to relieve his men at about 11.00 on 26 May and that written orders to that effect arrived soon afterwards from Guy Gough. He does not mention the Dorsets at all. What probably took place was a movement by the Dorset's D Company towards Gorre to plug the gap that appeared after the Lancashire Fusiliers withdrew from the line of the canal. The original position of the Dorset's B Company was in fact further to the east of Gorre, with A Company (Second Lieutenant John Peebles) on their left and C Company holding the line up to the bridge at Pont Fixe. Peebles would later join 5 Commando and died in a grenade accident in 1943.

Interestingly, the war diaries of both the Lancashire Fusiliers and Dorsets do mention the French ammunition train on the far bank of the canal opposite Gorre, the Dorsets' historian claiming it was their mortars that set it alight! What is far more likely is that the ammunition train was still smouldering after the Irish Fusiliers episode and any exploding ordnance was the direct result of the explosion precipitated by the Irish on 25 May.

110

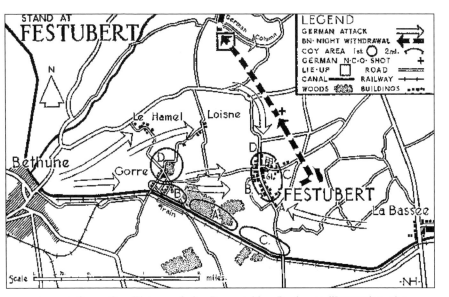

A map from the *History of the Dorsetshire Regiment* illustrating the battalion's withdrawal from the canal and their subsequent engagement at Festubert.

Nevertheless, the Dorsets were very conscious of the fact that that they were now fighting over the same ground the 1st Battalion had fought on during October 1914, twenty-six years previously, and were anxious not to disgrace themselves on the ground where fourteen officers and over 450 other ranks had died on this same stretch of canal. The battalion was commanded by Lieutenant Colonel Eric Stephenson, a remarkable individual who, at 48-years-of-age, had already been decorated with the MC and two bars for his gallantry with the regiment in the First World War. His tenacity and point blank refusal to surrender was about to write the battalion into legend.

Under heavy shelling and repeated attacks, the Dorsets, by this time reduced to a fighting strength of only 380 men, held their positions. Attacking them were men from two battalions of the 4th Panzer Division, supported by over twenty armoured vehicles. The Dorsets' only anti-tank defence was a handful of Boys anti-tank rifles but, despite their limited effectiveness, they managed to knock out several tanks. In a series of defensive battles the Dorsets won several decorations for gallantry as their rifle platoons held their ground and their Bren Gun Carriers were used to counter attack. The enemy, who had crossed the canal further west, were attacking the Dorsets' right flank. Among those decorated in these attacks were Captain Chips Heron, Sergeant 'Gary' Cooper and two Sergeant-Majors called Brown – Reg and Sid.

111

Meanwhile Bandsman Harold West, a Dorset stretcher-bearer, moved about under fire, tending the wounded and winning a Military Medal.

The 27 May opened with another heavy enemy assault on the Dorsets. Later in the morning Stephenson realized the situation was becoming desperate when a handful of Lancashire Fusiliers arrived with news that the battalion had been overrun. Reports had also come in that 1/Cameron Highlanders had been almost completely wiped out and that the 7/Worcesters on their left 'were none too happy'. With the enemy enveloping the Dorsets' right flank and the Argyll and Sutherland Highlanders machine-gun section destroyed to a man, Stephenson was more than a little relieved to receive orders to withdraw to Festubert, where the 1st Battalion had been billeted in October 1914.

With a textbook display of professional soldiering, the Dorsets disengaged and withdrew under fire to establish their new perimeter around the village; with them were the remnants of D Company, 7/Worcesters. Stephenson's plan was to hold Festubert by defending the four major approach roads: D Company to the north straddling the D116; B Company to the southwest holding the D72; A Company defending the southern approaches from the canal; and C Company the eastern end of the D72 and approaches from Violaines. Controlling the battle from battalion headquarters at the crossroads in the centre of the village, Stephenson barely had time to get his men into position before the first attack began at 4.45pm. Infantry supported by six armoured vehicles assaulted the C Company sector but were driven off with the loss of one light tank. Regrouping, the enemy then switched their attack to B Company with nine tanks which, from all accounts, proved to be a 'hectic action' as the tanks were driven off again by the remaining 25mm anti-tank guns, Boys rifles and Bren guns. As the enemy withdrew towards Gorre they left eight of the Dorsets' carriers burning and one destroyed anti-tank gun.

With dusk approaching, the B Echelon transport attempted to break out to the north but ran headlong into a German armoured column, the few surviving vehicles managing to return to the perimeter. Time was

There is much evidence to suggest that good field craft was practised and taken seriously by the Germans. The soldier in the photograph is armed with an MP 40 Submachine gun and had used local vegetation to break up the line of his helmet.

now running out for the Dorsets as D Company came under attack from six armoured vehicles, one firing straight down the Rue des Cailloux. Major Bob Goff, already wounded from a previous attack, continued to lead D Company as they withdrew into an orchard 'with both sides firing point blank at each other until the Boche decided to pull out'. The final attack came shortly after 7.00pm which, although repulsed, convinced Stephenson the time to break out had arrived.

A lesser individual may well have considered surrendering the battalion at this point but, far from beaten and determined to outmanoeuvre his enemy, Stephenson took the decision to lead his surviving men across country to Estaires – a march of about ten miles. At 9.30pm fifteen officers and 230 other ranks – all that was left of the battalion – and a collection of other men from various regiments, assembled south of the village. With Stephenson in the lead and Major Tom Molloy as his assistant navigator, the battalion moved south of the village across the fields before heading northwest to cross the D72. On one occasion they shot a German NCO who had discovered them and on another they waited with baited breath until a German column had passed; but each time fortune was on their side and they escaped unscathed. At 2.30am they found themselves on the banks of the canalised River Lawe, a water obstacle they had to cross twice as their route took them unwittingly across a large bend. Tired, wet and triumphant, they arrived at Estaires at 5.00am on 28 May. It had been another impressive chapter in the long history of the regiment and one that was rewarded by Stephenson's DSO, which was announced in October 1940. The battalion was evacuated from Dunkerque to Margate on 30 May, courtesy of a Thames dredger:

The sight of this unwieldy craft, which, as first seen in the dark, was apparently half filled with water, had so appalled Major Sam Symes [B Company] *when he had been sent forward with the advance party, that he had refused to take it over. It was explained to this harassed officer that this was the normal condition of dredgers and actually the craft was quite seaworthy.*

B Company 2/Manchester Regiment
Commanded by Major E M Hickey, B Company was attached to 5 Brigade and deployed around Violaines, a little to the northwest of La Bassée, the war diary reporting that movement was made all the more difficult by the absence of large scale maps. As with the other companies of Manchesters, Hickey's men shared the fortunes of the brigade to which they were attached. Number 7 Platoon was overrun by German tanks at

Gorre and, in attempting to get in touch with them, Major Hickey was taken prisoner. Number 6 Platoon was shelled out of its first position early on 27 May and their last message was that was that enemy tanks were drawing in. Very few of B Company were in a position to withdraw when the order was received.

7/Worcestershire Regiment

The battalion moved from Mouchin on the Gort Line to billets in scattered farmhouses north of Givenchy, arriving on 24 May. The battalion was under the command of 46-year-old Lieutenant Colonel John Parkes, a man who had risen from private soldier in 1914 and was commissioned in the field shortly after being awarded the DCM in 1916. In 1929 he left the army in the rank of major to begin ten years of civilian life before being recalled in 1939 to take command of the 7/Worcesters. He died in 1967 and his name is commemorated on the north wall of the nave of St Mary and All Saints Church, Kidderminster.

No.	Corps	Name
2563	1/7 BN WORCS Rgt	PARKES
SGT	(TF)	J

Operations		Vol.	Page	
DCM	LG	14·1·1916	A 23	
	AO	1-4·1916	A 28-56	

The medal index card of Sergeant John Parkes, showing the award of the DCM in 1916. He was commissioned a short time later. Parkes was evacuated from Dunkerque with the survivors of the 7/Worcesters.

Having been ordered to take up positions along the canal, the Worcesters moved into position after dark along a two and a half mile frontage running from Givenchy in the west to the western edge of La Bassée. Parkes deployed D Company, under Captain John Tompkinson, on the right flank, where contact was made with C Company, 2/Dorsets, on the left flank. A Company held the centre ground while C Company were in touch with the Camerons.

Warning signs that the Germans had already crossed the canal came when the commanding officer's vehicle came under fire, wounding Major Richard Goldie, the battalion's second in command, and the Intelligence Officer, Second Lieutenant Woodward. As it transpired later, both A and C Companies had already been overwhelmed and, despite a counter attack by the two platoons of B Company, no headway was made. During this time Major John Boyt's A Company lost three of its platoon commanders, Patrick Monahan, Sam Ibbetson and David Goodwin, who was killed while trying to contact the company on his right.

Captain John Tomkinson commanded D Company in May 1940.

As dusk fell on 26 May, John Parkes and his battalion were in considerable difficulty. Enemy tanks were showering the Worcester's positions with high explosive shells and the casualty rate was increasing by the hour. The battalion was badly situated along the canal and had practically no effective field of fire, observation was non-existent and enemy aircraft were continually flying over the battalion's positions during the hours of daylight and, despite sending out runners, there had been no information from A and C Companies. The next morning, a strong force of enemy infantry and tanks crossed the canal on the D Company front opposite Givenchy.

The officers and NCOs of D Company, taken in 1939 before the battalion moved to France. In the front row (L to R) are: Sergeant Warr, Lieutenant Lord Coventry, Captain Williams, Second Lieutenant Hunt and CSM White.

115

Withdrawing under fire to Givenchy with about seventy men, Captain John Tompkinson and his depleted company held the village until 3.30pm, before withdrawing with the survivors to Festubert with the 2/Dorsets. Amongst the D Company casualties was Lieutenant Lord Coventry.

The memorial to Lieutenant Lord Coventry in the Church of St Mary Magdalene at Croome.

IN LOVING MEMORY
OF
GEORGE WILLIAM REGINALD VICTOR
10TH EARL OF COVENTRY
BORN 10TH SEPTEMBER 1900
KILLED IN ACTION IN FRANCE 27TH MAY 1940

As for the remainder of the battalion, the orders to withdraw came almost too late for the majority. Two carriers remained behind to cover the withdrawal and what remained of the battalion retired towards Lavantie where transport took them to le Doulieu. Of the original Battalion, which marched into Belgium with twenty eight officers and nearly 700 other ranks, twelve officers, including John Parkes, and 354 other ranks were evacuated from Dunkerque on 31 May.

1/Queen's Own Cameron Highlanders

The battalion was under the command of 43-year-old Lieutenant Colonel George Miller, who had been commissioned into the regiment in December 1915. Awarded the MC in 1916, he was appointed to command the 1st Battalion in September 1939. The 1/Cameron Highlanders were said to have the distinction of being the only regiment in the BEF to wear the kilt in battle and some were still wearing it as they were marched off into captivity. However, there is photographic evidence to suggest the men from 4/Cameron Highlanders and 1/Gordon Highlanders in the 51st (Highland) Division were also wearing the kilt in May 1940 and were certainly taken prisoner whilst wearing it.

After their withdrawal from the Escaut, the battalion arrived in Violaines at 6.30am on 24 May and were ordered to relieve the 1/7 Queen's on the canal, which they did at 11.00pm on 25 May. Miller deployed his men along a line that ran approximately from the western edge of La Bassée to Salomé, with B Company on the right, D Company in the centre, covering the crossing points, and C Company on the left. Miller kept A Company in reserve at Battalion Headquarters in Violaines. Even at this early stage Captain Ronnie Leah, commanding B Company, was concerned that his men continually failed to get in touch with C Company of the Worcesters on their right flank, agreeing with the rather pessimistic outlook voiced by his French counterpart that the situation looked a little grim!

German infantry crossing the canal.

It quickly became obvious that the enemy had crossed the canal in the gap between the Worcesters and Leah's company, and were evidently attempting to work round the right flank – at this point there was no report from the Worcesters as to the demise of their C Company. A counter attack at 1.30am on 27 May by Major Riach and A Company appeared to stop the infiltration; but in the cold light of day, machine-gun fire from positions described as 'being in front of the Worcesters left hand company' indicated a considerable enemy presence had crossed the canal and A Company were once again instructed to drive the enemy back across the canal. This time the two platoons of A Company, consisting of forty five officers and men, were supported by six French tanks from the 1st Division Légère Mecanique (Light Mechanised Division) and although the attack was initially successful, the heavy casualties and sustained fire from the far bank made it increasingly impossible for A Company to hold their ground. After withdrawing, only eighteen men of A Company returned to Violaines and, of these, only six were left unwounded. Riach was awarded a DSO for his leadership during this attack.

Once a bridgehead had been established, German forces crossed the canal using pontoon bridges. Here a Panzer (38t) crosses the canal with its crew, while another waits its turn. A sunken barge can be seen in the background.

Prisoners from the 1/Cameron Highlanders are seen here assisting in the construction of a pontoon bridge. Although it was forbidden to force prisoners to engage in war related work in the front line, there was little that could be done to prevent it.

Orders to withdraw from the canal arrived at lunchtime on 27 May. Captain Ronnie Leah was at D Company HQ when the news arrived:

A runner suddenly arrived with a verbal message from the CO to the effect that the Camerons were to withdraw immediately. We commenced to withdraw about 1.45pm but not with a great deal of hope, as we knew the enemy were round on both sides and probably behind us.

The only accounts we have concerning the fate that befell the three forward companies are the personal diaries of Ronnie Leah, Captain Donald McBrayne (C Company) and CSM Mackintosh (D Company). According to the battalion war diary, orders were not sent out until 3.15am on 27 May, which is at odds with Leah's account. However, the diary is correct in its assertion that D Company managed to get a small handful of men away but C and D Companies were 'unable to get even one man away'. Leah's diary records Second Lieutenant Mainwaring and PSM Kerr heading across country with a group of men, mainly from 10

119

and 11 Platoons, minutes before several tanks forced the main party to take refuge in a ditch:

Had got about 300 yards when confronted by several tanks and had to get down in the field and available ditches. In my ditch were the remains of the original 10 Platoon, Sergeants Turner and Watson, Privates Leidlar, Gillespie, Nicholson, Buchanan and Elvin. Opened fire on tank with the Bren and unfortunately the anti-tank rifle jammed and the strike broke. The ditch was very uncomfortable, with about one foot of water in it.

Exhausted and soaking wet, Leah and his party were eventually captured while trying to break through the German outpost line at Laventie. The final entries in the war diary, which was clearly written up after the event, are concerned with the fortunes of Battalion HQ and the remnants of A Company at Violaines. At this stage they were in danger of being outflanked by the Germans. The Cameron's had little artillery support to speak of until the brigade anti-tank platoon of three 25mm guns arrived under Second Lieutenant Duncan Callander to reinforce the defensive flank. Corporal Walker of A Company recalled that the farmhouse in which Battalion HQ was situated was soon ablaze:

Second Lieutenant Duncan Callander in the dress uniform of the Cameron Highlanders.

Second Lieutenant Callander scored hit after hit on the German armour ... They kept on firing, though the drifting smoke from Givenchy obscured their view ... When almost surrounded a dispatch rider succeeded in reaching them, and gave them their orders, but C and D Companies were caught in the trap and none of them got out. Callander's anti-tank platoon, with a score of twenty-one tanks to its credit, followed the carriers and the remnants of A Company across country.

Callander's MC was gazetted in December 1940 but Ronnie Leah was taken prisoner with the majority of the battalion and ended his war in Colditz Castle, retiring in 1947. At Dunkerque around 100 officers and men, all that remained, were evacuated from the East Mole.

Chapter Nine

The Tours

The northern section of the Canal Line, running from Gravelines down to Aire sur-la-Lys, is only a short distance from the Channel Ports and is easily explored, either on the way to a visit to the First World War battlefields, or as a detour on the return journey. The southern section, which includes Béthune and La Bassée, is only some five miles south of Neuve Chapelle and the First World War battlefields of French Flanders. In fact, the canal was the scene of fighting in both world wars and in at least one case the same regiment found themselves fighting on the same ground their fathers had fought over twenty six years earlier.

There are four car tours that take in the whole of the Canal Line from Gravelines to La Bassée and, while I have not included maps for these tours (the IGN Série Bleu 1:25000 maps are more than sufficient), all four offer the battlefield visitor the opportunity to engage in short walks. However, I have drawn maps for two of the walking routes, which allow the visitor to explore the area in more depth. The author strongly suggests obtaining street maps from the various Tourist Offices along the route to supplement your excursions and, while much of the area covered by the guide is dotted with cafés and other refreshment venues, it is always wise to have something to eat and drink with you.

Maps
As mentioned above, the tours described in this book are best supported by the IGN Série Bleu 1:25000 maps, which can be purchased at most good tourist offices, in the bigger local supermarkets and online from www.mapsworldwide.com. However, bear in mind that satellite navigation can be a very useful supplement in supporting general route finding, particularly when trying to locate obscure CWGC cemeteries. The Michelin Travel Partner Map can also be downloaded free onto your iPad. There is much to be said for making preparations for your visit in advance by using Google Earth or *Geoportail*, the French equivalent, to explore the area online.

Travel and where to stay
By far the quickest passage across the Channel is via the Tunnel at

Folkstone, the thirty six minutes travelling time comparing favourably with the longer ferry journey from Dover to Calais or Dunkerque. Travelling times vary according to traffic; but as a rough guide the journey from Calais to Gravelines via Marck and Oye Plage is about half an hour, while the journey from the ferry port at Dunkerque to Gravelines is around fifteen minutes. Calais to St-Omer via the A26 is about forty-five minutes and around fifty minutes from Dunkerque via the D928.Whether your choice of route is over or under the Channel, early booking is always recommended if advantage is to be taken of the cheaper fares.

If you are intending to base yourself in the north, the author can recommend the **Hostellerie Saint Louis** at Bollezeele, which is situated in a small village north east of Watten. The hotel is closed on Sundays but boasts an excellent restaurant. The rooms are a little basic but very clean and comfortable. It is wise to book well in advance: hostellerie saintlouis@gmail.com. A little further south, St-Omer has a number of hotels, including the 3-star **Hotel le Bretague**, which is near the railway station and a ten minute walk to the main square and the Saturday market. Alternatively, the 3-star **Hotel Ibis**, on Rue Henri Dupuis, is situated in the heart of the town and has parking at the rear. However, there are a host of hotels and self catering gites available through the Gites de France and Logis Hotels websites.

For those of you who prefer campsites, **Camping Château de Grandspette** at Éperlecques is an ideal and attractive venue. In addition to the usual pitches for tents and caravans, the site has mobile homes and fully equipped tents for hire and boasts a swimming pool, restaurant and bar, as well as wifi. Further information on all aspects of accommodation can be obtained from the various Tourist Offices in the main centres at Gravelines, St-Omer and La Bassée.

Driving

Driving abroad is not the expedition it was years ago and most battlefield visitors these days may well have already made the journey several times. However, if this is the first time you have ventured on French roads there are one or two common sense rules to take into consideration. Ensure your vehicle is properly insured and covered by suitable breakdown insurance; if in doubt contact your insurer, who will advise you. There are also a number of compulsory items to be carried by motorists that are required by French law. These include your driving licence and vehicle registration documents, a warning triangle, a *Conformité Européenne* (CE) approved fluorescent safety vest for each person travelling in the car, headlamp beam convertors and the visible display of a GB plate.

Whereas some modern cars have built in headlamp convertors and many have a GB plate incorporated into the rear number plate, French law also requires the vehicle to be equipped with a first aid kit and a breath test kit. If you fail to have these available there are some hefty on the spot fines for these motoring offences if caught driving without them. Most, if not all, of these items can be purchased at the various outlets at the Tunnel, the channel port at Dover and on board the ferries themselves.

Driving on the 'wrong side of the road' can pose some challenges. Here are three tips that the author has always found useful:

1. When driving on single carriageway roads try to stop at petrol stations on the right hand side of the road. It is much more natural then to continue driving on the right hand side of the road after you leave. Leaving a garage or supermarket is often the time when you find yourself naturally turning onto the wrong side of the road.
2. Take your time! Don't rush! If you rush your instinct may take over and your instinct is geared to driving on the left.
3. Pay particular care on roundabouts. A lot of drivers do not or rarely appear to use indicators. Navigators, remember to look at the signs anti-clockwise and drivers remember that the danger is coming from the left.

On a more personal note it is always advisable to ensure that your E111 Card is valid in addition to any personal accident insurance you may have; and have a supply of any medication that you may be taking at the time.

Visiting Commonwealth War Graves Commission Cemeteries
The CWGC cemeteries visited in this guide are generally to be found in churchyards or in communal cemeteries, such as **Renescure Communal Cemetery,** although you will find British casualties from 1940 located in a number of existing First World War Cemeteries, such as **Longuenesse Souvenir Cemetery** at St-Omer and **Aire Communal Cemetery,** north of Aire-sur-la-Lys**.** Remember, further details of all the casualties in the larger cemeteries will be found in the cemetery register, while others will be lodged with the cemetery guardian and not easily accessed.

Visitors should remember that where a soldier has been recovered from the battlefield it is not always possible to identify exactly when he was killed or died. To that end on some headstones the CWGC has provided two dates between which it is presumed the individual died. When visiting the fallen from the Second World War along the Canal Line, it is impossible not to be constantly reminded of casualties from the First World War, the numbers of which probably horrified the men of the BEF who fought in this area during May 1940. The visitor will also come across the graves of aircrew that were shot down over the course of the war and those men who died during the advance in 1944 after the D-Day landings. The graves of men killed in the area during May and June 1940 are probably the least visited in the whole of France. The small numbers of men, whose headstones are almost lost amongst the French civilians in communal cemeteries, are all but forgotten. One cemetery that stands out is the **Bleue Maison Military Cemetery** near Éperlecques, where there is a single unidentified British soldier from 1940 buried amongst the sixty First World War casualties. Visitors to the area should ensure that these soldiers and airmen are not ignored and make a point of visiting their often isolated graves..

The concept of the Imperial War Graves Commission (IWGC) was created by Major Fabian Ware, the volunteer leader of a Red Cross mobile unit that saw service on the Western Front for most of the period of the First World War. Concern for the identification and burial of the dead led

The familiar green and white sign denotes the presence of British war graves. French casualties are marked in a similar fashion while German cemeteries are marked by black lettering on a white background. Note that some communal cemeteries such as this at Meurchin have opening and closing times.

him to begin lobbying for an organization devoted to burial and maintenance of those who had been killed or died in the service of their country. This led to the Prince of Wales becoming the president of the IWGC in May 1917, with Ware as his vice president. Forty-three years later the IWGC became the Commonwealth War Graves Commission (CWGC). The Commission was responsible for introducing the standardized headstone, which brought equality in death regardless of rank, race or creed and it is this familiar white headstone that you will see now in CWGC cemeteries all over the world. Where there is a CWGC plot within a communal or churchyard cemetery the familiar green and white sign at the entrance, with the words *Tombes de Guerre du Commonwealth* will indicate their presence. French military cemeteries are usually marked by the French national flag and those which are contained within communal cemeteries are often marked by a sign at the cemetery entrance bearing the words: *Carré Militaire, Tombes de Soldats, Morts pour la France.*

Car Tour 1

Gravelines to Watten

Start: Oye-Plage Communal Cemetery
Finish: The Blockhaus d'Éperlecques
Distance: Twenty miles
Maps: IGN 1:1000,000 Lille-Bologne-sur-Mer 101
            IGN 1:25, 000 Dunkerque 2302O
            IGN 1:25, 000 Watten 2303O

The Communal Cemetery at Oye-Plage is best approached via the A16 and the D940 from Marck to Oye-Plage. You will find details of the cemetery at the end of this section. After leaving the cemetery, continue along the arrow straight D940 for three miles to take the D11A towards Gravelines. Just as you pass over the narrow Rivière d'Oye you will notice the Cochon Noir Monument on your right, marked by several

The Cochon Noir Monument.

126

flagpoles. If you stand with your back to the monument and look across to the flat ground on the far side of the road you will be looking at the area – Cochon Noir – where many of the Belgian civilians were killed.

Leave the monument and continue along the D11A, go straight on at the point where the main road bends round to the right, and park near to the disused bridge. This is the old swing bridge on the Calais road that Lieutenant Allen identified in his notes as Bridge 1.

You will see from the large rocks barring the way onto the bridge is no longer in use but in May 1940 it was the scene of considerable fighting by French and British troops as the armoured vehicles of the 1st Panzer Division attempted to cross into Gravelines. It was this bridge that the Belgian civilians endeavoured to cross on 23 May and was used by Major Bill Reeves and his four tanks from 3/RTR to cross into Gravelines after their escape from Calais. Second Lieutenant Armstrong and K Troop of 3/Searchlight Regiment defended the bridge, along with Second Lieutenant John Hewson and 13 Platoon of the Green Howards. Hewson was killed here firing a Boys anti-tank rifle.

Bridge 1 on Rue de Calais taken from the ramparts.

Return to your vehicle and turn right along Quai Ouest, keeping the marina on your left. After the road bends round to the left, continue for 160 yards to see a small parking place on the right where you can leave your vehicle. Cross over the road with care and step over the barrier by the bridge.

This is Bridge 2, as identified in Lieutenant Allen's notes, and can still be walked across using the former roadway, from where there is a good view of Bridge 1. This bridge and the railway bridge were defended

Bridge 2 on Quai Ouest at Gravelines.

by Lieutenant Dunn's J Troop. The road you have just crossed bends round to the left to span the canal via a new road bridge, which was built much later.

After returning to your vehicle, continue across the canal via the new road bridge and follow signs for Centre Ville, which will lead you into Place Albert Denvers via Rue de Calais, where there is plenty of parking. Drivers should be aware that there is a rather quaint one-way system in operation within the town, but parking is free between 12.00 and 2.00pm

Once you have parked in Place Albert Denvers you will find the Tourist Office in **Rue de la Republique**, a useful venue where you can obtain a street plan along with a map of the ramparts walk. Parking is difficult here on Fridays owing to the market taking up most of the square. Visitors should be warned that it is not possible to walk completely round the ramparts and the route – less than two miles – does involve a section that lies east of the town, before finding its way back to the Arsenal, via Rue Andre Vanderghote.

At the opposite end of **Place Albert Denvers** you will see the imposing gates of the Arsenal; by crossing the bridge and following the pathway to the ornamental Arsenal Gardens, it is possible to get an excellent view of Bridge 1 from the ramparts. If you clamber up the grassy bank that borders the gardens, the view across to the bridge is the same as the crews of the French 75mm guns would have had when the bridge was approached by the armoured vehicles of the 1st Panzer

The entrance to the Arsenal at Gravelines.

Division. Two further visits should be considered before leaving Gravelines; the first is the communal cemetery at les Huttes and the second is the memorial to the Hardtack 11 Commando raid that took place in December 1943.

Les Huttes Communal Cemetery

This large cemetery is situated on the Rue de Dunkerque. With the cemetery on your right, park your vehicle near the bus stop by **Rue Béguinage**. Here, to the left of the entrance gate, along the perimeter wall, are a number of the Belgian civilian graves from the Cochon Noir disaster. The grave of **Philemon Timerman** is at the end of the row but

The plaque is erected over the graves of Belgian civilians killed on Cochon Noir.

his wife is probably buried in one of the many unknown graves. Above the gravestones is a plaque placed by the civilian authorities in Gravelines in memory of the Belgian dead.

The Commando Memorial
This memorial can be found on **Route de l'Aquaculture** on the edge of the dunes, not far from the present day power station. The objective of Hardtack 11 was to make a reconnaissance of the beaches and dunes east of Gravelines and finally went ahead on the night of 24/25 December 1943. The party consisted of five Frenchmen from **10 (Inter-Allied) Commando**, commanded by Warrant Officer Wallrand, and two men from 4 Commando, Sergeant John Parkes, the dory's coxswain, and the Russian born Corporal Jones, the dory signaller. Their task was to lie offshore in the dory and await a signal to pick up the raiding party. The party were taken just offshore by motor torpedo boat (MTB) from where they carried on to the beach by motorized dory. The landing was successful but the dory was eventually abandoned after it was swamped,

The Commando Memorial to the men of Hardtack 11 on Route de l'Aquaculture.

A motorized dory of the type used by the Hardtack 11 Commando Raid.

drowning Parkes and Wallrand. By this time another signaller, called Chapman, had joined the party from the offshore MTB and, with all hopes of rescue dashed, the party made their way inland. Jones and Chapman were taken prisoner but the remainder made their way inland and joined the resistance.

Leave Gravelines on the D11B and cross over the railway line just west of the swing bridge (Bridge 3). The road follows the line of the River Aa before it becomes the D218 and takes you to into Saint-Folquin, where you head east along the D 218. After 0.65 miles, having passed over one crossroads, you come to a second crossroads; go straight across here and follow the D229 Route de Bourbourg to the canal.

The bridge you can see is Bridge 4, which is marked **Pont du Bac** on the IGN Série Bleue maps, and was known in 1940 as the bridge at **Les Targette**. This was the bridge defended by Lieutenant Boycott and L Troop, together with two French 75mm guns from 402nd Régiment d'Artillerie. You will have arrived on the German 'side' of the canal and a short walk across the bridge will give you the view that Boycott and his men had on 22 May 1940. The high bank referred to by Boycott, where he positioned Bombardiers Blair and Patterson, is probably in the vicinity of the wooded area to the north of the bridge. As you stand by the bridge, imagine Bombardier William Gilbert crossing the canal by boat, armed with two cans of petrol, which he sprinkled over the wooden swing bridge in an unsuccessful attempt to set it alight. The advanced units of 1st Panzer Division crossed the canal at this point on 24 May.

With the canal on your left, drive south along the narrow road for two miles to reach the bridge at St-Nicolas.

Bridge 4 at Les Targette has been replaced by a modern lifting bridge.

The modern bridge at St-Nicholas is similar to that at Les Targette.

You will have again arrived on the German side of the canal. Very little is known about the defence of this bridge, apart from a note in Lieutenant Boycott's account that the bridge was under the command of a party of Green Howards and the officer commanding the party informed Second Lieutenant Trist, who was in temporary command at Les Targette, that he had been ordered to withdraw.

Continue south with the canal on your left for 1.9 miles to reach the bridge at St-Pierre-Brouck. At the junction turn right and cross the canal and park where convenient.

The **1/Super Heavy Battery** arrived on the canal on 23 May with orders to strengthen the French unit that was already in situ. You are parked on the British side of the canal and the single French 75mm gun would probably have been positioned a little further back on the D110, **Rue de Bistade**. One can imagine Major Henry Boxhall's frustration when the French gunners retired on 24 May, leaving their gun and four rounds of ammunition, soon after the first German units appeared on the other side of the canal. By 11.00am on 24 May the Germans were across the canal and the battery withdrew.

Keeping the canal on your right, continue south to Holque. The bridge is south of the town at le Ruth and 190 yards north of the TGV Bridge. This is the crossing point mentioned by Guderian in his book *Panzer Leader*.

The bridge was not one that had been allocated to Usherforce and was apparently defended by a battalion of the 137th Regiment of Infantry, who held out against the 4th Panzer Reconnaissance Battalion until they were forced to retire to the Haute-Colme Canal.

Continue under the TGV railway line on the D3B and pass under the footbridge which has replaced the former railway line. In a further 250 yards you will pass beneath the bridge carrying the D300, bear left and turn right at the junction, following the D3 over the bridge. This route will eventually take you to the Grand Place, where you will see a signpost for the D26 – Wulverdinghe and Merckeghem – on your left. Follow the one way system which will take you along the D26 onto the heights above Watten. Park by the farm and ruined abbey.

After leaving your vehicle, walk across the road for a fine view over Watten below you. You are standing on the so-called Wattenburg Heights, which was the scene of the attack by the SS-Division *Leibstandarte* Adolf Hitler (LSSAH) on 25 May. Commanded by *Obergruppenfüher* Sepp Dietrich, the attack was noteworthy as it directly contravened the terms of the Hitler Halt Order but still earned Dietrich the Iron Cross First Class. Guderian writes of the attack in *Panzer Leader*:

> *Early on 25 May I went to Watten to visit the Leibstandarte and to make sure they were obeying the order to halt. When I arrived I found the Leibstandarte engaged in crossing the Aa. On the far bank was Mount Watten, a height of only 255 feet, but that was enough in this flat marshland to dominate the whole surrounding countryside. On top of the hillock, among the ruins of an old castle [sic], I found the divisional commander, Sepp Dietrich. When I asked why he was disobeying orders, he replied that the enemy on Mount Watten could look down the throat of anybody on the far bank of the canal. Sepp Dietrich had therefore decided to take it on his own initiative. The Leibstandarte and the Infantry Regiment Gross Deutschland on its left were now continuing their advance on Bergues and Wormhout. In view of the success they were having I approved the decision taken by the commander on the spot and made up my mind to order the 2nd Panzer Division to move up in their support.*

You should be able to see the tower of the 11th century ruined abbey at the far end of the farm buildings; it was in these ruins that Guderian met Sepp Dietrich. The windmill was restored in the 1990s.

Retrace your steps downhill to Watten, turning left onto the D213 to cross the bridge. After crossing the canal, turn left and park alongside the river on the left.

The ruined abbey on the heights above Watten.

The station building at Watten remains much the same as it was in May 1940, apart from the rather obvious alterations.

The road bridge at Watten defended by 3/Super Heavy Battery.

You are now on the German side of the canal and looking across to the British positions. On 23 May Second Lieutenant Cocks and his troop were dispatched by Major Percy Strudwick, commanding **3/Super Heavy Battery**, to the bridge. On hearing that German armoured vehicles were within three miles of the bridge, Strudwick reinforced the garrison. A French unit took up position on the main road – presumably the D3 – and on the Wattenburg Heights and came under fire from German mortars situated in the railway station yard. The first LSSAH attack on the bridge began just after midnight on 24 May, after which Cocks and his men retired to **les Moëres**, leaving the defence of the bridge to the French units, a defence which apparently crumbled some hours later when the LSSAH crossed the canal.

To find the railway station, continue along the D213 – Route de Saint-Omer – for approximately 180 yards, keeping the canal on your left. Turn right into Rue de la Gare – you will also see a CWGC signpost for Bleue Maison Military Cemetery directing you along the same road. The railway station is 200 yards further along on the left.

The station yard is where German mortar teams established themselves and bombarded the Wattenburg Heights. Despite the post war building, there are still good views to be had of the hill and, on a clear day, it is possible to see the remains of the abbey. The station building remains much as it was in May 1940, although recent modernization has left its mark!

After leaving the station car park, turn left along the D207 and cross straight over the roundabout. Continue for almost a mile and take the turning on the right – Rue des Sarts. By this time you should have picked up signposts directing you to the Éperlecques bunker.

The V1 and V2 Blockhaus d'Éperlecques
This can be treated as an optional visit as it is not part of the 1940 landscape. However, the sheer size of the installation, where some of the most offensive weapons of the Second World War were constructed, will inevitably make an impression on the visitor. This is certainly one of the, if not the, largest bunkers in the north of France and, built with slave labour from the occupied countries, it still bears the effects of British and American bombing. Some seventy five feet high and covering an area of two and a half acres, it was initially planned to be the launch site for the V2 but after heavy Allied raids, it became the manufacturing plant for the V2's rocket fuel. The site has been open to the public since 1973 and listed as an ancient memorial in 1985. The entrance fee at the time of writing is ten euros and opening times are as follows:

The entrance building to the museum and blockhouse at Éperlecques.

A small part of the huge blockhouse at Éperlecques. A German halftrack can be seen bottom right.

April and October, 10.00am to 6.00pm,
May to September, 10.00am to 7.00pm
March and November, 2.15pm to 5.00pm
Annual closing from December to February.

Cemeteries
Oye-Plage Communal Cemetery

Situated on the D940 from Calais, a right turn at the traffic lights in Oye-Plage – where a CWGC signpost on the left directs you to the cemetery – will take you to the car park on the right. The British war graves are in the top right hand corner, marked by the Cross of Sacrifice, where you will find sixty one identified casualties and over forty unidentified, many of which were brought in post war by the Army Graves Service. Buried here are eight identified soldiers from the 4/Oxford and Buckinghamshire Light Infantry (Ox and Bucks), three of whom were definitely at Cassel during the rearguard action and were killed during the breakout on 30 May 1940. 36-year-old **Major Geoffrey Wykham** (Row 2, Grave 22) had transferred from 1/Ox and Bucks in March and took over HQ Company; 27-year-old **Second Lieutenant Colin Dillwyn** (Row 3, Grave 19) was the Battalion Intelligence Officer and 33-year-old **Captain Lucian Falkiner** (Row 3. Grave 15) was in B Company. It is more than likely that a number of the remaining men of the Ox and Bucks, and the six other ranks from 2/Gloucesters, were also victims of the breakout from Cassel. This action is detailed in the Battleground Europe volume *Cassel and Hazebrouck 1940*. In Row 5, Grave 15, you will find 30-year-old **Sergeant John Park**, who was drowned on Christmas Day 1943, during the Hardtack 11 Commando Raid east of Gravelines. **Lieutenant Donald Carpmael** (Row 1. Grave 13) and **Lieutenant Kenneth Gurr** (Row 1, Grave 14) were flying a Swordfish Mark 1 from 812 Fleet Air Arm Squadron when they were shot down over the Calais-Gravelines road on 24 May 1940. Although a long way from Dieppe, 23-year-old

Oye-Plage Communal Cemetery.

137

Marine John Mackinstry (Row 1, Grave 8) was one of twenty two casualties sustained by 40 Commando on19 August 1942. Of the five RAF casualties, four are victims of the 1940 battles. **Pilot Officer Cecil Montgomery** (Row 1, Grave 19) and **Flying Officer Peter Collard** (Row 1, Grave 10) were both flying Hurricanes from 615 Squadron when they were shot down over the Channel on 14 August 1940. **Flight Lieutenant Wilfred Harris** (Row 1, Grave 16) was washed up on the French coast after his 214 Squadron Wellington crashed into the sea. The crew of five were never recovered. It was a similar story with 24-year-old **Sergeant Bernard Westhorp** (Row 1, Grave 11). His 44 Squadron Hampden crashed into the Channel on 10 September 1940; sadly, his body was the only one of the crew of four that was recovered. **Flying Officer David Goulden** (Row 2, Grave 4) was washed ashore on 20 May after his 550 Squadron Lancaster crashed into the sea on 10 May 1944. Three crew members are buried in Dunkirk Town Cemetery and the remainder are commemorated on the Runnymede Memorial. In March 1945 HMTS *Alert* left Plymouth for repair work on the La Panne submarine cable and was torpedoed in the Channel. Three of the crew members were subsequently washed up at La Panne, 33-year-old **Second Officer James Dixon** is buried in Row 5, Grave 6, while 46-year-old **Chief Engineer, Herbert Fisher** (Row 5, Grave 18) and 30-year-old **Fourth Officer John Taws** (Row 2, Grave 5) are buried close by. A memorial plaque commemorating the *Alert* and its crew was unveiled at Broadstairs Harbour in 2012.

Bleue Maison Military Cemetery

If you are visiting the railway station at Watten, turn left after leaving the car park and continue along the D207 towards Éperlecques. Cross over the roundabout and take the next turning on the left, the cemetery is 400 yards further along this road on the left hand side. There is one unidentified soldier from 1940 buried here amongst the sixty identified casualties from the First World War. He was brought in from Oye-Plage Churchyard and could be one of the Green Howard casualties from the action around Gravelines, although quite why his remains were not reinterred at Oye-Plage Communal Cemetery remains a mystery.

Car Tour 2

St-Momelin to Aire-sur-la-Lys

Start: The bridge at St-Momelin
Finish: Aire Communal Cemetery
Distance: Twenty-five miles
Maps: IGN 1:1000,000 Lille-Bologne-sur-Mer 101
IGN 1:25, 000 Watten 2303O
IGN 1:25, 000 St-Omer 2304O
IGN 1:25, 000 Aire-sur-la Lys 2304E

Although I have recorded a distance of twenty five miles from St-Momelin to Aire, the visitor may well choose a shorter or longer route depending on their circumstances and, to that end, I have not provided precise details of the route. The tour begins at the bridge at St-Momelin, which can easily be reached along the D213 from Watten. Once in the village there is plenty of parking opposite the château. The bridge was defended initially by **8/Searchlight Battery** and then **52/Heavy Regiment,** Royal Artillery, under the command of Lieutenant Colonel

The château at St-Momelin where Lieutenant Colonel Comerford established his headquarters.

139

Augustine Comerford. The château that Comerford requisitioned as his headquarters still stands as it was in May 1940 and, although access is limited, the building can be seen from the bridge and the access road down to the canal. The deserted factory referred to in the 52/Heavy Regiment war diary is no longer in existence, neither is the cafe on the opposite side of the canal, from where the Germans established a mortar team. Comerford and his mixed group of units left their positions during the early hours of 25 May, leaving the French garrison to hold the bridge. To reach the Churchyard Cemetery follow the D928 to the T-junction with the D326 taking the first road on the left towards the church.

After leaving the cemetery your next stop is the **railway station at St-Omer**. As you enter the town via the D928, Quai du Haut Pont, you will pass the house where Wing Commander Douglas Bader was discovered after he had escaped from the Clinique Sterin in Rue St-Bertin. (See **Walk 1** for further details). There is convenient parking by the canal on Quai du Commerce, close to the station.

The magnificent station building is still intact although much of it is not in use. The view from the bridge, which crosses the canal from **Quai du Commerce**, has been downgraded to some extent by the recent additions of two restaurants. However, as you walk over the bridge to the station building you cannot help but be impressed by the grandeur of the building. The bridge was defended by Captain Wilfred Bickford and No 3 Company of the Don Details and it was here that the E2 gun from Major Cubitt's 392/Battery had been sent before it was redirected to Hazebriouck by a staff officer. There is no doubt that Bickford would have held out for a longer period if the gun had been positioned here. Captain Ernest Hart

The railway station building at St-Omer, seen from the bridge that was defended by Captain Bickford and 3 Company, Don Details.

and his convoy of 9/Royal Northumberland Fusiliers were most probably directed by French soldiers into the centre of St-Omer on 22 May over the level crossing on Rue du Metz. Whether these soldiers were in fact Germans wearing French uniforms is debatable but the demise of Hart's column followed after they were ambushed in the town.

Longueness Airfield
The airfield is south west of St-Omer and just over half a mile from the cemetery at Longuenesse. The airfield is seen as the birthplace of the Royal Air Force, as it was here that the Royal Flying Corps established their first base in France and, for the duration of the First World War, was the largest and probably the most important airfield on the Western Front. In recognition of the importance of the airfield, the British Air Services Memorial was unveiled here in September 2004 by Air Chief Marshal Sir Brian Burridge and Lieutenant Général Jean Gaviard of the French Air Force. It was designed by Tim O'Brien for the Cross and Cockade Aviation Historical Society. Amongst the more well known pilots that operated from here were Captain John Liddell, Major Billy Bishop, Major Mick Mannock, Major Geoffrey Bowman and Captain Cecil Lewis. Up until 23 May 1940, when St-Omer saw the arrival of the German Army, the airfield was again used by British squadrons, before it eventually became home to German fighter squadrons supporting the German air offensive against the United Kingdom.

The British Air Services Memorial at Longuenesse.

The *Cross and Cockade* bas-relief on the rear of the Air Services Memorial.

141

Arques Churchyard Cemetery.

In May 1940 there was no by-pass round St-Omer and the road led straight to Arques, which was a town in its own right. Today the two conurbations have expanded to join each other. North of St-Omer the canal is known as the Canal de l'Aa while to the south it becomes Canal de Neufosse. As you leave St-Omer on the D210 you will soon come to Arques Communal Cemetery, which is next to the church at the junction of **Rue Adrien Danvers** and Avenue de la Liberation. Turn right at the roundabout and park in the cemetery car park.

Our next stop is **the bridge in Arques**. After leaving the cemetery retrace your steps to the roundabout and turn right towards the canal. The modern day bridge at Arques is situated on the D210, Avenue Pierre Mendèz France, the result of the short by-pass that was built after the war to avoid the centre of Arques.

Arques is where 228/Field Company suffered a number of casualties after a premature explosion killed and wounded some of 2 Section. To reach the bridge, continue along the D210, where there is a road on the left, just before the bridge, leading down to the canal. The road swings round to the left and continues under the bridge, find a convenient parking place on the right. In May 1940 the bridge was some 300 feet further south and the visitor can easily spot its position from the two roads that are now separated by the canal. Second Lieutenant Dakin and his detachment of 9/Royal Northumberland Fusiliers were deployed to hold the railway bridge, visible from the bridge at Arques, which you can reach by continuing alongside the canal for another 700 yards. This is also the site of the Fontinettes boat lift, which was completed in 1888. The lift was used by canal traffic until 1963 before the new lock – L'écluse des Fontinettes – was built further upstream.

The building on the western bank of the canal at the site of the former bridge at Arques is still recognizable today.

Exactly where the E3 Gun from 392/Battery was positioned is unclear but, after the gun and its crew withdrew, Cubitt ordered the gun to immediately return to Arques, by which time the canal had been crossed by the Germans. The war diary tells us the gun came into action at a crossroads east of Arques, which would place it in the vicinity of Fort Rouge on the D210. It was from this area that Major Andrew Horsburgh-Porter and A Squadron of 12/Lancers rescued the gun and its crew.

The bridge at Renescure (Pont de Campagne) is on the D200 and can be approached via Blendecques and Campagne-lès-Wardrecques or, if you do not wish to visit the churchyard cemetery at Campagne-lès-Wardrecques, by continuing across the canal at Arques on the D211 and working your way east of the industrial estate to find the D200.

The modern day road bridge at Renescure.

The bridge was the scene of 58/Chemical Warfare Company's attempt to demolish the bridge using a lorry load of explosive. Apart from the sappers, the garrison consisted of 6/Battery from **2/Searchlight Regiment** and the E4 Gun and crew from **392/Battery**, which was positioned some 200 yards east of the bridge on the D200. The gun destroyed two houses on the opposite bank and an enemy armoured vehicle before it was incapacitated.

The village of **Renescure** is another one and a half miles to the east along the D355. As you approach the village you will see the church, marking the position of the cemetery.

Next to the cemetery is the **Château de Zuthove**, where Major Ifan Lloyd established the headquarters of 58/Chemical Warfare Company and where Driver Albert Hardy returned after the company had withdrawn, hoping to find two members of the company who were missing.

From Renescure the D406 will take you to the crossroads with the D255, where a left turn will take you to a car park on the left, just before the bridge. This is **the bridge at Wardrecques** and although the village of Wardrecques is on the far side the canal and another 1.2 miles to the west, the bridge is referred to in war diaries as the bridge at Wardrecques.

This is where the F1 gun from **392/Battery** was positioned in support of the French infantry and the men of 6/Battery, **2/Searchlight Regiment**,

The Château Zuthove at Renescure.

under the command of Lieutenant Doll. The bridge was blown on 23 May. The F1 gun was hit and disabled by German mortar fire before the British garrison withdrew to Bergues.

The quickest way to reach the **bridge at Blaringhem** is to cross the canal and take the left turning along Chemin du Halage for 1.8 miles. This canal side road is narrow but will take you straight to the bridge.

There was a considerable garrison defending this bridge, consisting of British and French units. The F2 gun from **392/Battery** was deployed here under the command of Lieutenant Kenneth Payne. During the withdrawal the gun was lost and Second Lieutenant Groombridge and some of his detachment of **2/Searchlight Regiment** were badly injured

The road bridge at Blaringhem, where Second Lieutenant Keith Payne commanded the F2 gun from 392/Battery.

145

after the Germans forced a passage across the canal by using some of the sunken barges.

From Blaringhem, cross the bridge and after 200 yards, turn right at the crossroads along the Rue de Neuffosse. This narrow road continues along the side of the canal to reach a fork in the road. Bear right here to reach **the bridge at Garlinghem**.

The bridge, although referred to as the bridge at Wittes, is actually at Garlinghem. The village of Wittes is to your right on the other side of the canal. After reaching the bridge, cross over the canal and turn left onto the D197E2, drive for 180 yards down to Rue de l'Argent and park. In May 1940 the bridge in question spanned the canal from here across to Chemin de Neuffosse, which you can see on the far side and was where HQ Section of **228/Field Company** recorded a premature explosion on 22 May. The three men killed in this mishap are buried in Aire Communal Cemetery. The F3 Gun from **392/Battery** was also deployed here but little is known of its fate and the crew was eventually taken prisoner.

Retrace your steps back across the bridge and drive down the D157E3 to the junction with the D157. Turn right and, after 600 yards, stop by a small road on the left – Rue de la Becque Saint-Georges.

This is the approximate spot where Second Lieutenant Hook and No 2 Platoon from 9/RNF were taken prisoner after the rescue mission carried out by the 5/Royal Inniskilling Dragoon Guards on 24 May.

Looking up the D157 towards Boëseghem at the approximate spot where Second Lieutenant Hook and 2 Platoon, 9/RNF were taken prisoner.

Continue along the D157 in the direction of Aire-sur-la-Lys and cross the canal over the road bridge, which was blown by 228/Field Company. Continue, over two intersections, for 700 yards and then turn right onto the D192, signposted Wittes and St-Omer. Continue to the roundabout, from where you should be able to see Aire Communal Cemetery on your right.

Our tour ends here but the author strongly suggests you take time to visit the town, which boasts, amongst other architectural and cultural attractions, the magnificent Collegiate Church of Saint-Pierre and the Jesuit Chapel of Saint-Jacques. The Tourist Office can be found in the triangular shaped Grand Place, where there are numerous cafés and eating places.

The road bridge on the D157 at Aire-sur-la-Lys was blown by 228/Field Company.

Cemeteries
St-Momelin Communal Cemetery
From the bridge turn left onto the D326, the first turning on the left – Rue de la Mairie – will take you to the church. The churchyard contains two 1940 graves, which you will find on the right by the boundary fence. 30-year-old **Corporal Stanley Aries** was married to Doreen and was

St-Momelin Communal Cemetery.

147

killed serving with 9/RNF on 25 May and was more than likely a member of 6 Platoon, commanded by Second Lieutenant Ross. **Gunner William Macdonald** was 40-years-old when he was killed on 25 May, serving with 52/Heavy Regiment. Judging from the dates on the CWGC database it is likely his body was not recovered until after his unit had withdrawn.

Longuenesse (St-Omer) Souvenir Cemetery

This is a large cemetery, containing 3177 identified casualties from both World Wars and is accessed from the D928. The author recommends using the car park on Rue Louis Delatre, avoiding the sometimes hazardous crossing of the main road. The cemetery takes its name from the triangular cemetery of the St-Omer garrison, which is located behind the Cross of Sacrifice and contains eleven rows of French graves. As you walk through the First World War graves, ponder for a moment the closeness of some of the headstones; the men here were more than likely buried side by side in mass graves.

Longuenesse Communal Cemetery.

There are 342 identified graves of men killed during the Second World War, of which 188 were killed or died serving with the BEF; a large number were brought in from the surrounding battlefields during and after the war. Five men from the 4/Ox and Bucks that were killed during the breakout from Cassel are in Plot 8, Row A, which is close to the far wall near the main road. **Privates Norman Chamberlain** (Grave 49) and **Edward Hughes** (Grave 54) and **Lance Corporals Alfred Carter** (Grave 42) and **Guy Langfor**d (Grave 30) are buried close to **Second Lieutenant Charlie Clerke Brown** (Grave 46), who commanded the battalion's carriers. Badly wounded in the blockhouse at le Peckel while serving with 8 Platoon, 2/Gloucesters, was **Lance Corporal Dennis Ruddy** (Grave 53). Deployed just north of Cassel by Lieutenant Colonel Gilmore, Ruddy was taken prisoner along with the remainder of his platoon when Second Lieutenant Roy Cresswell surrendered on 30 May. Ruddy died of wounds in captivity.

Amongst the gunners from the Royal Artillery buried here in Plots 8 and 9 are several men who were involved in the 140 Brigade stand at Cassel and Hazebrouck. Plot 9 is behind the Cross of Sacrifice and is where you will find **Gunner Reginald Manning** (9.A.20) from 5/Royal Horse Artillery, who was badly wounded at Hondeghem and subsequently died of his wounds on 27 May. Two men from 7/Royal Tank Regiment are buried side by side. Australian born **Captain Herman Kauter** (8.B.6), the battalion's Adjutant, and **Trooper Henry McGillivray** (8.B.7) were both killed on 21 May, during the Arras counter stroke. The five men from 140/Field Regiment were most likely killed during the breakout from Cassel and were possibly in **Major Edward Milton's** (9.A.4) group; similarly, the four men from 98/Field Regiment may well have been casualties from the Hazebrouck breakout. Details of this engagement can be found in the Battleground Europe publication, *Cassel and Hazebrouck 1940*. The five men from 57/Anti-Tank Regiment were most likely involved in the fighting on 24 May, when Brigadier Gawthorpe launched his counter attack from Aire. **Gunners Alfred Yorke** (Grave 26), **Fred Gainey** (Grave 28), **James Poplett** (Grave 29), **Reginald Grandfield** (Grave 36) and **James Alkinson** (Grave 41) are all buried close together in Plot 8, Row A. 39-year-old **Private Arthur Todhunter** is the only member of the Tyneside Scottish buried here. He was killed during the ambush at Pronier Farm, Ficheux, and his body may well have been discovered some time after the 70 Brigade disaster, as the majority of those killed on that day are now buried at Bucquoy Road Cemetery and Mercatel Communal Cemetery.

The 2/5 Leicestershire Regiment, who relieved the 2/Essex on the Canal de la Deûle, were almost annihilated by the advancing German infantry. Four private soldiers, most likely men who died in captivity or who were killed attempting to reach Dunkerque, are also to be found here. **Privates John Summerfield** (Row C, Grave 49), 22-year-old **Tom Finney** (Row C, Grave 53) and 31-year-old **James Young** (Row C, Grave 54) are all to be found in Plot 8, while **Private Edward Roseblade** (Row A, Grave 22) is buried nearby in Plot 9.

You will also find a number of men who were killed serving with other formations along the line of the canal. **Second Lieutenant Peter Browne** (10.B.2) was second in command of B Company, Royal Irish

Fusiliers, when he was killed by mortar fire, along with his orderly, 24-year-old Fusilier James Ewart, who is commemorated on the Dunkirk Memorial. **Drummer George Cornwall** (10.B.46) of the 1/8 Lancashire Fusiliers was a member of the battalion that relieved the Irish Fusiliers and **Lance Corporal William Baggins** (10.A.13) was killed while serving with the 6/Green Howards, as was 20-year-old **Second Lieutenant John Hewson** (10.A.14), who was killed firing a Boys rifle near the bridge on the Calais road at Gravelines. 24-year-old **Lieutenant John Gregson** (10.A.3) died of wounds on 27 May at St-Venant, whilst in command of D Company, 2/Durham Light Infantry. Educated at Chetlenham and Sandhurst, he was commissioned in January 1936 and left a widow, Eleanor.

Captain John Gregson was killed at St-Venant.

Nearly ninety commonwealth aircrew, along with four Polish pilots, are buried here. Most are casualties of the post 1940 air war, but five are casualties from the air battles of 1940. Flying a Westland Lysander II from 16 Squadron, 29-year-old **Flight Lieutenant William Clapham** and his air gunner, 23-year-old **Sergeant Roy Brown,** were shot down by ground fire. Both men are buried in a joint grave in Plot 6, Row A, Graves 2 and 3. **Flight Lieutenant Charles Darwood** (8.B.31) was flying a Hurricane from 111 Squadron when he was shot down by Me109s south of Mons on 18 May and **Pilot Officer Peter Ranier** (10.A.20) was one of two pilots from 145 Squadron lost while flying Hurricanes over Dunkerque on 27 May. **Pilot Officer Horace Scott** (10.A.19) was the air gunner in a Defiant I flown by Flight Lieutenant Edward Whitehouse when they were attacked by Me109s off Ostend. Shortly after the battle commenced their aircraft was seen to crash into the sea. Scott was washed ashore and Whitehouse is commemorated on the Runnymede Memorial. A sixth member of the RAF, **Leading Aircraftsman Archie Lockwood** (10.B.31), was part of the crew of Seaplane Tender ST243, which was sunk in the Channel on 2 June 1940 during the Operation Dynamo evacuation from Dunkerque. Two other victims of Operation Dynamo were 40-year-old **Chief Engine Room Artificer Horace Millard** (10.B.24), who was killed aboard HMS *Keith* when she was sunk on 1 June 1940 while rescuing British troops from Dunkerque and 28-year-old **Able Seaman Alfred Hammond** (10.B.25), who was among the nineteen crew and 275 troops that were killed when HMS *Skipjack* was sunk on the same day.

Arques Churchyard

The cemetery is on the western bank of the canal at the junction of Rue Adrien Danvers and Avenue de la Liberation, with the car park at the western end, just off Avenue de la Liberation. After entering through the main gate, the British graves can be found on the left side, just before the church and marked by a large union flag. There are six identified casualties and two which remain unidentified. Probably the most interesting burial here is **Captain John Hoare**, a British Overseas Airways Corporation pilot who was killed when the aircraft he was travelling in crashed near Arques. Hoare had been flying an Armstrong Whitworth Ensign, which had been destroyed on the ground at Merville by Me 109s, and was flying home in a DC3 from 24 Squadron when it was hit by anti-aircraft fire over Calais. The navigator was killed, two passengers were wounded and the pilot was shot attempting to reach French lines. The four Northumberland Fusiliers were all killed on 23 May and were possibly killed in the vicinity of the railway bridge, the defence of which had been entrusted to Second Lieutenant Dakin. The 2/Searchlight Regiment deployed 6/Battery to the bridge at Renescure, so it is reasonable to assume that 21-year-old **Gunner William Dando** of 6/Battery was killed in the vicinity on 23 May.

Campagne-lès-Wardrecques Churchyard

The churchyard cemetery is just over half a mile from the bridge and is situated on the D200. There is plenty of parking and the British graves are at the rear of the church. There are three identified casualties here from the Second World War, all killed in May 1940, and three from the previous conflict. **Lance Bombadier Norman Buttigieg** and **Gunner John Hunt** were both serving with 6/Battery, 2/Searchlight Regiment and **Fusilier Thomas Moore** was serving with 9/RNF.

Renescure Churchyard

The church is in the centre of the village and there is ample parking near the Château de Zuthove. Keeping the church on your right, the British graves are on the left as you enter the cemetery. There are nearly twenty graves from the Second World War, of which fourteen are identified. The three men from the 1/East Riding Yeomanry (Royal Armoured Corps) were more than likely members of C Squadron, who were ordered to send out a patrol to the Fôret de Clairmarais on 26 May 1940. The war diary tells us that Second Lieutenant Hopper, who was commanding 4 Troop, bumped into the enemy when approaching the Fôret de Nieppe, losing two carriers and four men. At least three of the four men of 6/Battery, 2/Searchlight Regiment, were part of the bridge garrison at Renescure

The entrance to Renescure Communal Cemetery.

but there is a question mark over **Lance Bombardier Norris Lewis**, who was killed on 20 May. The two men of the 9/RNF may have been part of the detachment that was left at Arques under Second Lieutenant Dakin. The memorial plaque to **Driver Albert Hardy** is also here, situated between the headstones, although at the time of writing it was suffering from the effects of weathering.

Lynde Churchyard
The village of Lynde is situated on the D55 Ebblighem to Steenbecque road, with the churchyard in the village centre. There are three burials here, of which one is from May 1940. Interestingly, all three men were serving with cavalry regiments when they were killed, but our interest lies with 21-year-old **Second Lieutenant Andrew Roddick,** who was killed on 23 May serving with the12/Lancers. His death occurred during the A Squadron reconnaissance that enabled the majority of Major Cubitt's D Troop guns to escape from being overwhelmed. Major John Crichton, 5th Lord Erne, who was second in command of A Squadron and attached from the Royal Horse Guards, was so severely wounded in the skirmish that he died of wounds later. He is buried in Wormhout Communal Cemetery.

152

Aire Communal Cemetery

This large cemetery contains the dead of both world wars and can be found to the north of Aire-sur-la-Lys, just off the D943. There are 911 identified casualties buried here, of which there are eighteen identified men from 1940. The British graves are marked by the Cross of Sacrifice and you will find the men of the Second World War in two plots, either side of the cross. Here you will find three of the Royal Engineers from 228/Field Company who were killed during the premature explosion at the Garlinghem bridge at Wittes. **Captain Wilfred Middleton** (1.AA.5) and **Sapper Joseph Huntington** (1.AA.6) are buried side

Captain Wilfred Middleton.

by side, while **Sapper Cyril Moreland** (4.G.7) died of wounds the next day. Three more men from 228/Field Company lie nearby in Plot 4. **Sapper Harry Hadfield** (4. G.5), **Lance Sergeant Kenneth France** (4.G.6), and **Sergeant Albert Crapper** (4.G.9) were killed or died of wounds on 23 May. These men may have been victims of the second premature explosion at Arques.

Aire Communal Cemetery.

Car Tour 3

St-Venant

Start: Calonne-sur-la-Lys
Finish: The footbridge at Haverskerque
Distance: Eight and a half miles
Maps: IGN 1:1000,000 Lille-Bologne-sur-Mer 101
IGN 1:25, 000 Lens 2405E
IGN 1:25, 000 Hazebrouck 2404O

We begin at the communal cemetery in Calonne where the cemetery surrounds the church in the centre of the village; leave your vehicle in the car park situated just before the village war memorial in **Place de Souvenir.** The church, which was razed to the ground in the First World War, suffered the indignity again in 1940 when the belfry tower collapsed after being shelled. Twinned with Northiam in East Sussex, the village has seven panels sited at strategic points, providing a tour that takes in the church and cemetery, the station and former water mill. Calonne was where the 1/Royal Welch Fusiliers began their advance in the late afternoon of 24 May to take control of the four bridges spanning the canal near Robecq and from where the Carrier Platoon was sent forward to gain contact with the enemy, who were reported to be in St-Floris. Lieutenant Colonel Harrison ordered B Company to swing south from St-Floris to recapture the two bridges immediately south of Robecq, D Company initially to follow B Company and then move to the bridge east of the village, and A and C Companies to occupy the l'Epinette Bridge, after they had cleared St-Venant of enemy troops on 25 May.

Keeping the cemetery on your left, drive through Calonne, turning right then left through the bends in the road, to follow signposts for the D186 and St-Floris. Slow down as you approach St-Floris as on the right, opposite Rue Duriez, you will see a demarcation stone marking the line on which the German Lys offensive ran out of steam in 1918. Introduced in 1920

The demarcation stone at St-Floris.

by Paul Moreau-Vauthier, the original idea was to place a stone monument at every kilometre along the western front from Belgium to the French-Swiss border. Twenty four of these monuments were destroyed during the Second World War and today only ninety two remain intact. Continue to the church at St-Floris and park. The Second World War graves are outside the churchyard on the roadside next to the village war memorial; take care here as they are easy to miss. To the left of the war memorial, and erected in 1988, is the only commemorative monument to the men who fought in the 1918 Battle of the Lys. The church is where the Fusilier's Carrier Platoon first encountered resistance; a German anti-tank gun was situated initially at the road junction near the church but withdrew as the carriers forced their way up the main street.

The graves of the RWF at St-Floris are buried outside the churchyard.

Continue along the road for another eighty-five yards to where the road forks. C Company by this time had caught up with the carriers and as the carriers approached the fork in the road, the two leading carriers were knocked out by enemy anti-tank guns, killing the crews of both vehicles. It was here that **Lieutenant John Garnett** was killed, along with six of his platoon. The seven graves you have just visited are the

155

men who were killed on this spot on 24 May. [Garnett's grave stone records his death as 23 May but, as the RWF were not in St-Floris until the next day, this is unlikely]. Incidentally, Garnett's father commanded the 25th (Montgomery and Welsh Horse Yeomanry) Battalion of the Royal Welch Fusiliers in the First World War and one of his company commanders was the poet Siegfried Sassoon. It was at St-Floris in July 1918 that Sassoon was wounded in the head and invalided back to the UK.

Lieutenant Colonel Harrison, mindful of the onset of nightfall, decided to remain in St-Floris until the arrival of daylight would allow him to continue to the canal bridges. He was clearly unhappy about his situation, the battalion had only three maps of the area in its possession, to the south and west was an enemy of unknown strength and he had no idea how far the advance of the Royal Berkshires had progressed. Added to that, any enemy advance up the undefended Robecq-Calonne road, which was already under heavy shell fire, would cut the battalion's line of communication. St-Venant was occupied the next morning by A and C Companies after some opposition. The DLI reached Calonne on the morning of 25 May and that evening Lieutenant Colonel Simpson was ordered to occupy St-Venant in support of the RWF.

Continue along the D186 into St-Venant for half a mile until you come to a crossroads with a large factory building on the right and the tiny Chapelle Notre Dame de l'Immaculée Conception on the left. Turn right here onto the Rue des Amusoires, leading up to the canal.

In 450 yards you will reach the canal. The large building on the right is where the Taverne farm was situated in May 1940 and where Lieutenant Colonel Simpson established the DLI Battalion HQ, along with a 2-pounder anti-tank gun and crew. You can imagine the activity here as road blocks were erected and the gun crew were ordered to engage enemy armour over open sights. In the final moments of the defence, enemy tanks appeared from two directions and closed in on the DLI position. Before he was taken prisoner, Simpson was seen firing his revolver at the tanks and infantry coming towards him up the road and at least one tank was disposed of with a Boys rifle.

Follow the canal side road round to the left and park at the communal cemetery. Just to the right of the cemetery wall was where Lieutenant Colonel Harrison established his final command post, which was within crawling distance of Lieutenant Colonel Simpson's HQ. It is between the two battalion HQs that **Captain Cyril Townsend** crawled along the canal to Harrison's HQ to receive the news that Harrison intended to hold the bridge over the canal to enable some men to get across. The small wooded area to the right of the cemetery is where Harrison deployed the anti-

The canal side road looking from the communal cemetery towards the modern day road bridge and the Royal Welch Fusiliers' Memorial.

Lieutenant Colonel Harrison positioned his anti-aircraft platoon in the copse near the cemetery.

aircraft machine gun platoon, which was later deployed against the advancing Germans.

Continue along the towpath and pass beneath the new road bridge, stopping by the memorial you can see on the right. Dedicated at a ceremony in November 1997, the memorial commemorates the 1/RWF at St-Venant and stands close to the bridge across the Lys Canal, which proved so difficult to cross under enemy fire. The canal is currently bridged by the lock gates but a little further on the concrete supports of

The former road bridge is thought to have been constructed to the left of the present day lock.

The Royal Welch Fusiliers Memorial is positioned close to the former bridge spanning the Lys Canal.

the 1940 bridge can still be seen and aerial photographs taken just after the war indicate this where the original bridge crossed the canal. This is the point where Lieutenant Colonel Harrison was killed and Captain Clough-Taylor was taken prisoner. Captain Cyril Townsend managed to get across the bridge with some of the Durhams but by this time it was every man for himself as German armour smashed its way along and across the canal. If you stand at the lock gates with the RWF Memorial behind you, you have the same view that the beleaguered men of the RWF and DLI had when attempting to cross the canal. Sadly, for many it remained a bridge too far.

Our next stop is the former railway station. Leave the site of the bridge and, after passing the town war memorial on the right, head towards the church. (Visitors possessing a satnav will find it especially useful here.) You are now driving towards **Rue de la Gare** which is a *cul de sac* off Rue de Paris. After turning down Rue de la Gare, park near the former station building. The building is now a music and community centre and is where **Captain Clough-Taylor** organized a defensive position. If you walk round to the far side of the station you can see the line of the former railway – which at the time was on a raised embankment – and the water tower. **Lieutenant Colonel Harrison** established a command post on 25 May just south of the tower before moving to the communal cemetery. The railway line was where *Leutnant* Wallenburg of *8 Kompanie* II/IR 3 was killed with 7 *Kompanie*, using the water tower as temporary shelter from the hail of fire being directed on them by the defending men of the RWF.

The former railway station at St-Venant is now a music and community centre.

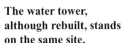

The water tower, although rebuilt, stands on the same site.

A short walk towards the road – which is blocked by large boulders – will take you to the former level crossing where **Major D I Owen**, the RWF second in command, redirected the wayward fusilier companies to line the railway embankment. German artillery often put down a blitz barrage on the level crossing and casualties here included **PSM Albert Evans** and **Corporal Leonard Smithers**. The level crossing area was always considered rather unhealthy as any movement immediately drew enemy fire. It was from here that Harrison reorganized the battalion to defend a line running from the level crossing to the crossroads at the eastern end of the railway embankment. All four very much depleted companies were forward with A Company on the right, C and D Companies in the centre and HQ Company on the left – B Company were by this time cut off in Robecq. The line faced south and covered St-Venant and the bridge over the canal, across which ran the road to Dunkerque.

The former level crossing is still recognisable today.

The DLI war diary tells us that they took up a position next to the RWF with all four companies in the line facing south – A Company on the left and D Company on the extreme right flank. It is presumed that after the railway line in St-Venant was overwhelmed the RWF fell back to the canal where both battalions fought their last stand.

Retrace your steps to the main road and turn left onto Rue du Faubourg. After 150 yards your will come to a roundabout, go straight across here, following signposts for Guarbecque and Isbergues.

You are now driving along the D186. Aware of the gap that existed on the right flank between the Royal Berkshires and St-Venant, Simpson moved, what may well have been, a composite B and D Company to the right flank and it is likely they used the D186 to reach their positions. Under the command of **Lieutenant John Gregson**, who established his company HQ at the junction of Rue d'Aire with Rue de Hurtevent, the only other named officers on the right flank appear to be **Lieutenant John Bonham** from B Company, who was taken prisoner on 27 May, and **Lieutenant Jasper Rudd**, who escaped captivity and returned home via Dunkerque. The exact details of this deployment remain unclear but we must presume that the line of the road was held, albeit sparsely!

Lieutenant John Bonham.

After just over one mile you will come to a small crossroads; turn right here into **Rue Berthelotte**, and continue until you come to the bridge over the Guarbecque stream and park your vehicle.

This is thought to be the extreme right of the flank held by the DLI, with the 1/Royal Berkshires deployed somewhere to their right. You are looking at the bridge where **Private Luke Bowden** (D Company) along with **Private Ronald Ablett** were positioned on the left, in front of the stream, with

The bridge over the Guarbecque stream on Rue Berthelotte.

Lieutenant Jasper Rudd.

Private Tom Rodgers (B Company) on the other side of the road. Rodgers is said to have continued firing his Bren gun after all his comrades were either killed or wounded. During the battle the DLI must have withdrawn north of the stream and it was there that Rodgers was said to have been killed and Bowden was wounded and taken prisoner. According to Bowden's evidence, he witnessed the death of Rodgers and Ablett, who were apparently buried with others in a field just left of the junction with Rue d'Aire. There are, however, a number of inconsistencies in this story; first, Bowden failed to recognise the burial site in 2002 when he

Private Tom Rodgers.

returned to the scene of his action and secondly, Ablett, who is recorded by the CWGC as being killed on 27 May, was seen being carried from the battlefield on a stretcher. The question that immediately springs to mind is, if he was already dead why would he have been on a stretcher? Interestingly, his family were informed he had died of his wounds a week later, on 3 June 1940, and his name is now commemorated on the Dunkirk Memorial. However, we shall probably never know the answers to this little mystery but the account does illustrate how the passage of time often distorts the reality of a situation.

Nevertheless, we can be sure that this was the approximate area defended by the DLI and if you look to the left of the bridge you can see, what can only be described as the Private Tom Rodgers Memorial, now a rather scruffy framed information board, containing an account of the battle together with a rough map drawn from information provided by **CSM Martin McLane**. It is hardly a fitting tribute to the men of the DLI,

The Tom Rodgers Memorial.

162

who deserve a more permanent memorial, such as that erected by the RWF in St-Venant. The current 'memorial' was placed by the bridge in 2004 after the brother of Tom Rodgers finally convinced the CWGC that Tom's remains, and presumably those of the others buried in Rue d'Aire, were reinterred at the St-Venant Communal Cemetery in June 1942.

Leave the bridge and continue straight ahead to the junction and pause. The field ahead of you is where Tom Rodgers and his comrades were said to have been initially buried. The Lys Canal is a mere three quarters of a mile to the north and it may well have been across this field that the surviving officers and men of B and D Company withdrew to escape the advancing German armour. Turn right and drive along Rue d'Aire for approximately 0.70 miles to where Company HQ was positioned just before the junction with Rue de Hurtevent. Lieutenant Gregson may have chosen the farm on the left, some 150 yards from the road junction, as his Company HQ; but, sadly, he was mortally wounded on 26 May on Rue d'Aire and died of his wounds the next day. Visitors to Longuenesse (St-Omer) Souvenir Cemetery will be familiar with his grave.

At the road junction a very sharp left turn will take you onto Rue de Hurtevent and to the junction with **Rue de Bas Hamel**. Turn right here onto a narrow minor road until you reach the foot bridge over the Lys Canal. Park by the bridge and walk up to the canal; the former roadway can still be seen and this is site of the bridge over which the Royal Berkshires, and possibly some of the DLI, crossed the canal. The present day footbridge was built post-war. The village you can see in the distance is Haverskerque, where Lieutenant Colonel Harrison is buried in the British Cemetery. The tour ends here.

The bridge at Haverskerque is now a footbridge.

Cemeteries

Calonne-sur-la-Lys Communal Cemetery

There are four CWGC plots dotted around the cemetery. There was heavy fighting in the village during May 1940 and the Germans used the school as an aid post, burying any British casualties in the field behind the school. In 1942 the local inhabitants moved these bodies to the communal cemetery but, in the process of re-interment, the identities of many of these men became obscured. The cemetery now contains twenty-three burials from the Second World War, fourteen of which remain unidentified. Visitors will also find two officers from the First World War.

St-Floris Churchyard

Lieutenant John Garnett is buried at St-Floris.

The communal cemetery is behind the church but the British war graves are outside the cemetery and were buried by the roadside in 1940. Today they are to be found in the same spot, south east of the church, by the war memorial. Drive slowly as they are easily missed. There is parking by the church. The dates on five of the headstones – 23 May – do not tally with the dates provided by the RWF war diary and other official accounts, which record the action at St-Floris as being on Friday 24 May; one can only assume the CWGC is incorrect. 21-year-old **Fusilier Harry Clamp** from Abersychan presumably died of wounds on 26 May.

St-Venant Communal Cemetery

This is a large cemetery where you will find casualties from the First World War together with 177 from the Second World War. Sadly, forty of the men killed in 1940 men remain unidentified. This total includes ninety officers and men originally buried in a mass grave. From the entrance on the canal the CWGC plot is at the far end of the cemetery. There is another entrance near the Cross of Sacrifice, which is approached from the D186. Walking down from the canal you will find the first of the 1940 graves in Plot III, to the right of the Indian Army plot. At the far end of Row III.B you will find the headstone commemorating the death of 21-year-old **Private Tom Rodgers,** inscribed with the words 'believed to be buried in this cemetery'. Walking further on, past the French military graves, the remaining rows of 1940 headstones can be found in Plot IV, in front of the Cross of Sacrifice.

    Captain Hugh Hall (IV.D.4), serving with the 1/Royal Berkshires, was killed at the bridge over the Lys Canal at Haverskerque on 25 May

St-Venant Communal Cemetery.

and it is likely that **Privates Walter Fletcher** (3.B.32), **Stanley Tovey** (4.C.40) and **John Jackson** (IV.D.7) were also casualties from the same heavy German shelling.

Of the seventy identified men of the DLI, former Wellington College schoolboy **Second Lieutenant Hubert Peel** (IV.C.44) was serving with A Company when he was struck in the back by shrapnel on 26 May; he died later that day from his wounds. 25-year-old **Private George Davis** (III.B.34) was killed while trying to swim the Lys Canal with his brother Lance Sergeant Thomas Davis, who was transferred from 6/DLI. George Davis, a pre-war soldier of some seven years' service, was killed on 27 May, not, as is inscribed on his headstone, 21 May. His family were informed of his death in 1941 after his body had been recovered. His brother, Thomas, survived, only to be taken prisoner at Dunkerque.

Thirty one identified men of the RWF are buried here and of these 38-year-old **PSM Albert 'Buck' Evans** (IV.C.38) and 35-year-old **Corporal Leonard Smithers** (IV.C.42) were killed on 26 May at the level crossing in St-Venant. **Second Lieutenant Alfred Bowen** (IV.C.7), commanding 8 Platoon was killed while the RWF were advancing along the St-Floris road on 26 May, while **Captain Edward Parker-Jervis** (III.A.9), commanding C Company RWF, was killed on 27 May defending a house in St-Venant that had been surrounded by the Germans. **Second Lieutenant Frank Ewart-James** (IV.B.3A) was also killed on 27 May as the RWF withdrew from the railway line.

Haverskerque British Cemetery

Rue du Colonel HARRISON

This cemetery can easily visited from Haverskerque by following the D122 and the CWGC signposts until you reach **Rue du Colonel Harrison**. The cemetery is at the end of this single track road, where there is plenty of parking. The cemetery contains burials from both world wars and the twenty-seven Second World War burials can be found behind the Cross of Sacrifice. The most senior British officer is 43-year-old **Lieutenant Colonel Herbert Harrison** (EE.1), who commanded the 1/RWF and was killed by the canal bridge at St-Venant. He is buried close to five men from his regiment who were all killed between 25 May and 27 May 1940. 22-year-old **Second Lieutenant Roy Phillips** (EE.22) of the DLI was killed on 27 May and is buried with four of his men. Phillips was commissioned in March 1940 and was in all probability attached to the 6 Brigade staff, as he does not feature on the final officer return made by the battalion. Another officer who definitely was on the 6 Brigade Staff was 28-year-old **Captain Gerard Roberts** (EE.30). The former Charterhouse schoolboy was killed on 27 May and was the son of Lieutenant Colonel Gerard Roberts, who was killed in June 1916 while in commanded of 14/DLI. The seven Royal Air Force casualties are all from 100 Squadron and were killed when their Lancaster III crashed NW of Haverskerque on the night of 31 July 1944, after attacking the flying bomb storage depot in the Forêt de Nieppe. 34-year-old **Alfred Sinclair** (B.21), the mid-upper gunner, served under the alias **Sergeant R A Gale**.

Haverskerque British Cemetery.

Robecq Communal Cemetery

The cemetery can be found on the D64 Robecq to St-Venant road. At the far end of the cemetery, behind the crucifix, a row of twenty-one headstones includes nine identified casualties from 1940. **Private Robert Fenwick** was serving with D Company, 2/5 West Yorkshires, when he was hit by flying masonry during the demolition of one of the bridges over the canal. He was the first casualty sustained by the battalion. The casualties from the Royal Welch Fusiliers were more than likely men of B Company, killed during and after the company had been surrounded. You will find all the identified casualties in the cemetery also have their names inscribed on the Robecq Memorial near the church.

Mont-Bernanchon British Cemetery

Situated on the D937 at the junction with the D184, a grass pathway between a house and a field leads down to a cemetery that contains 168 First and Second World War burials. Parking can be difficult although it may be possible to park on the nearby verge. The two 1940 Royal Norfolk Regiment casualties are to be found behind the Cross of Sacrifice and were probably casualties from the fighting north of the canal.

Mont-Bernanchon Churchyard

The church is in the centre of the village and there is ample parking nearby. The Cross of Sacrifice marks the CWGC plot, containing thirteen casualties from the First World War and fifty-five from the Second World War. Sadly, of these, an incredible thirty-three remain unidentified. The identified 1940 casualties are mainly men from the Royal Norfolk Regiment and Royal Scots, 4 Brigade, who were probably killed during the fighting north of the canal around le Cornet Malo and le Paradis. One can presuppose that many of the unidentified were killed in the same area. 24-year-old **Private Stanley Pryke** of the 4/Ox and Bucks remains a mystery, as his battalion was not near the canal at all. It can only be assumed he was killed during the breakout from Cassel on 29 May and was later brought into the cemetery, hence the 'between' dates.

**Mont-Bernanchon
Churchyard Cemetery.**

167

Car Tour 4

Festubert to La Bassée

Start: Festubert
Finish: La Bassée Communal Cemetery
Distance: Seven and a half miles
Maps: IGN 1:1000,000 Lille-Maubeuge 102
IGN 1:25, 000 Lens 2405E
IGN 1:25, 000 Hénin-Beaumont 2505O

This tour looks a little more closely at 5 Brigade area, who were positioned along the canal from Gorre to Salomé. The canal frontage allocated to the 2/Dorset's ran from just east of Gorre to Pont Fixe on the D166, and it was along the towpath, either side of Pont Fixe, that the first battalion fought in October 1914. The Dorsets were ordered to withdraw from the canal in the afternoon of 27 May, with the instruction to 'hold Festubert unless attacked, when you will withdraw fighting'. A fighting withdrawal can be a costly business but from all accounts the Dorsets were fortunate to withdraw relatively intact.

Lieutenant Colonel Stephenson ordered D Company to make for the northern end of Festubert and B Company to establish themselves on the southern exit to the village. It appears that D Company made the move without too much difficulty, although Major Sam Symes, commanding B Company, had some difficulty extracting his men from the canal bank, after being forced to withdraw across the enemy frontage. With the arrival of A and C Companies, which were east of Gorre along the canal, Stephenson completed his perimeter defences centred on the staggered crossroads at Festubert. It is likely that Colonel Steve, as he was known to his men, positioned himself at the crossroads, near, or in the basement of l'Église Notre-Dame.

The first enemy attack with infantry and six armoured vehicles came from the direction of the D166 at 4.45pm and was directed at C Company, who were positioned in the south east sector of the perimeter. With help from B Company the attack was driven off with the loss of one light tank. The next attack came from the direction of Gorre along the D72 and was levelled at B Company, this time with nine tanks. The armoured attack was beaten off by a mixture of Boys rifles and two 25mm anti-tank guns,

168

The staggered crossroads at Festubert where Lieutenant Colonel Stephenson organized the defence of the village. The CWGC signpost you can see in front of the private house is directing you to the Post Office Rifles Cemetery along the D72 to Gorre. The road running straight ahead is Rue des Cailloux, while the church is to the right of the picture.

while Bren guns stopped the infantry from gaining a foothold. But it was not without cost – apart from the inevitable casualties, one anti-tank gun and eight carriers had been put out of action.

About this time the battalion's transport attempted to get through the perimeter using the D166 towards l'Epinette. Initial elation turned to desperation as the column ran into enemy armour and, after a rather one-sided fire fight, only two or three vehicles managed to return to Festubert. As these vehicles returned to the crossroads enemy armour was close behind, launching an attack on the D Company positions with six armoured vehicles, firing straight down **Rue des Cailloux**. The company's one remaining Boys rifle was knocked out almost immediately, prompting Major Bob Goff, the company commander, to move his men into a nearby orchard. For the next fifteen minutes an intense close quarter fire fight took place with opposing sides firing almost point blank at each other. Fortunately, the Germans were the first to withdraw, possibly because a fourth attack from the direction of Gorre was already underway. On this occasion the attack was by infantry alone and, once again, the Dorsets held their ground, supported by the one remaining carrier possessed by the battalion.

After four attacks in two and a half hours and completely surrounded by an aggressive enemy, it would be only a matter of time before the survivors were overwhelmed. Incredibly Colonel Steve took the decision to march out across country and assembled his men in the fields somewhere to the south of the present day Rue du Trottin. It was from here that the survivors embarked on their cross country night march. Visitors may wish to visit **Brown's Road Military Cemetery** and the **Post Office Rifles Cemetery** before leaving Festubert, in order to get an impression of the ferocity of the fighting around here during 1914-15.

Leave the village on the D166, signposted Violaines, Givenchy and Cuinchy and continue over the five way intersection (Guard's Windy Corner Cemetery to the right) to **Pont Fixe**, or, as it is known today, Pont du Cuinchy. Pass over the bridge and park near the *Mairie* on the right.

Pont Fixe as it is today.

Walk back over the bridge and look along the canal to your left; this was the area defended by 2/Dorsets, while to your right the canal was defended by 7/Worcesters. Return to your vehicle and turn right along the D16 and after 500 yards turn left along Rue Julian Clement, passing **Woburn Abbey Cemetery** on your left. This cemetery is composed entirely of First World War casualties. Continue to the junction and turn left into Rue Emile Basly, to find **Cuinchy Communal Cemetery** on the left.

Leave the cemetery and retrace your steps over Pont Fixe, back to the five way intersection and turn right along the D167 towards Givenchy, signposted Givenchy and Violaines.

170

As you enter Givenchy–lès-La-Bassée, bear in mind that this village was the scene of not only the last stand made by D Company, 7/Worcesters, on 25 May 1940, but also the scene of 164 (North Lancashire) Brigade's heroic defence of the village on 9 April 1918, when the Victoria Cross was awarded to **Second Lieutenants Joseph Collin** and **John Schofield**. Both men are buried at Vieille Chapelle New Military Cemetery. Further details of this action can be found in *The Battles of French Flanders* by Jon Cooksey and Jerry Murland.

The Worcester's deployment along the canal put Captain John Tompkinson and D Company in touch with the 2/Dorsets on the right flank, although where exactly his positions were remain rather vague. Certainly his withdrawal into Givenchy allowed him to pull out with the Dorsets to Festubert on 27 May, where he presumably joined Lieutenant Colonel Stephenson on the night march to Laventie. He and the remnants of D Company were still with the Dorsets when they were evacuated from Dunkerque on 30 May. It does appear that official recognition of Tomkinson's leadership of D Company was overlooked, particularly as others in the same position received decorations for much less. Little more of his territorial career is known apart from the award of the Territorial Decoration in 1946.

Continue through Givenchy until you see the imposing 55th Division Memorial cross situated on a sharp right angled bend in the road; park to the right of the memorial on the minor road leading down to the communal cemetery.

The memorial was erected in 1921 but it was not until eighty-nine years later, in June 2010, that the long overdue Tunnellers' Memorial, with the story of **William Hackett VC** on an adjacent information board, was erected on the western edge of the plot. After visiting the two memorials, walk down the minor road for 65 yards to **Givenchy Communal Cemetery**.

The 55th Division Memorial at Givenchy. The communal cemetery is situated to the right of the memorial along a minor road.

171

Return to your vehicle and drive towards Violaines on the D167, passing the 55th Division Memorial on the right. Turn right at the water tower along the D167E, signposted La Bassée. At the next junction turn left and, after 150 yards, take the left fork to Violaines Centre. Violaines Communal Cemetery is straight ahead on the right, where there is plenty of parking.

From **Violaines Communal Cemetery** follow the road through Violaines to the D947, where a right turn will take you straight into La Bassée. As you enter the town it is impossible not to notice the St-Vaast church tower, which in this case is straight ahead of you. Follow the road and keep a sharp lookout for a signpost directing you to the *Cimetière* along Rue de l'Égalité, which you will find on the left hand side of the road. Although the tour concludes here, it is possible to continue to the Salomé waterfront and find some of the positions garrisoned by the 2/Essex Regiment and the 2/5 Leicesters along the Deûle Canal. However, the visitor will find themselves navigating through a rather unattractive urban industrial area.

Cemeteries
Cuinchy Communal Cemetery
The cemetery can be found on Rue Emile Basly, with the main British plot marked by the Cross of Sacrifice. Amongst the First World War graves are the men who fought in the local action that saw **Lance Corporal Michael O'Leary** win the Victoria Cross in February 1915. The Second World War plot is to the right of the entrance. Here you will

Cuinchy Communal Cemetery.

172

find five identified men from 2/Dorsets and one man from 7/Worcesters. 32-year-old **Corporal John Shanks** (1.B.9) was married to Edith and lived in Bournemouth when he was killed on the canal on 26 May, along with **Privates Ronald Price (**1.B.4), **Fred Preece** (1.B.6) and **Fred Damon** (1.B.10), while 21-year-old **Private George Charlwood** (1.B.2) most probably died of wounds on 28 May. Another mystery is 21-year-old **Private Cyril Jewkes (**1.B.3)**,** who is listed on the Worcestershire Regiment Roll of Honour as having been killed at Genval near La Hulpe in Belgium but, according to the CWGC, he died between 16 and 23 May. This makes it more likely he may have been injured on 22 May at Bruyelle and died in a nearby field ambulance.

Givenchy-lès-La-Bassée Communal Cemetery
The thirty-three Second World War headstones are in two rows to the left of the entrance, of these thirteen are unidentified. Apart from 19-year-old **Private Harry Bebber/Webber** (B.13) of the Dorsets, 30-year-old **Private George Coffield** (A.10) of the Cameron Highlanders and **Soldier Carpov** of the Russian Army, the remaining seventeen identified men are all casualties from 7/Worcesters. Three platoon commanders from A Company are buried here; **Second Lieutenants David Goodwin** (B.8), **Patrick Monahan** (B.12) and **Samuel Ibbotson** (A.8) were all killed on 26 May. The 39-year-old **Lieutenant George Coventry** (A.2) was killed serving with D Company on 27 May and it is not unreasonable to assume that a number of the men buried here were also part of the D Company defence of the village. George Coventry inherited the title of Earl of Coventry when his father, the 10th Earl, died in March 1930. 20-year-old **Private Leonard Sabin** (B.7), was born in Kenilworth, Warwickshire, and killed, according to the CWGC database, between 22 and 27 May 1940; however, on 22 May the

George Coventry, taken in 1930.

battalion was still on the Escaut at Bruyelle, making it more than likely he met his death on the canal. Sabin's name is also inscribed on the Kenilworth War Memorial in Warwickshire. The visitor will also find the date of death of a number of other casualties equally vague, such as that of 23-year-old **Lance Corporal Arthur Turner** (B.16), whose death has been recorded as taking place between 21 May and 2 June 1940.

Violaines Communal Cemetery.

Violaines Communal Cemetery

The village saw bitter fighting during May 1940 and at the time casualties were buried along the canal bank and in the surrounding fields. In 1942 local people transferred the bodies to the communal cemetery and there are now thirty Second World War burials here, of which three are unidentified. As one would expect, the vast majority are officers and men of the 7/Worcesters and Cameron Highlanders. The two men from the Queen's Royal Regiment are **Second Lieutenant Thomas Moore,** who was shot dead by one of his own sentries on 22 May; and **Private William Rutherford**, who was killed the next day. We can be reasonably sure that the thirteen men of the Worcesters were all killed on the canal or during the defence of Givenchy. Of the eleven men of the Cameron Highlanders, seven were killed on 27 May, either during the A Company counter attack or during the withdrawal from the canal. 19-year-old **Corporal William Buchanan**, of the 6/Argyll and Sutherland Highlanders, was probably another victim of the withdrawal from the canal and may well have been a member of one of the machine gun platoons that supported the Worcesters.

La Bassée Communal Cemetery

Rue de l'Égalité is a cul-de-sac and there is plenty of parking by the entrance to the cemetery. From the entrance walk up to the large crucifix and turn right, to find the small CWGC plot near the entrance on Rue des Fosses. Amongst the French and Belgian graves is a single row of Second World War graves. Seven men from the Cameron Highlanders lie next to four drivers from the Royal Army Service Corps, who, in many instances, were the unsung heroes of the campaign, transporting men and materials to and from the front line. Amongst the small number of civilian graves nearby are two that bring the full horror of the German occupation to the fore. **Gérard Detroix** and **Leon de Neys** were both shot by the occupying forces in September 1944 for being members of the French resistance.

The entrance to La Bassée Communal Cemetery.

Nearby Cemeteries
Salomé Communal Cemetery
There are two men from the Cameron Highlanders situated near the entrance, both killed on 26 May and both probably casualties from C Company, who were deployed at Salomé.

Provin Communal Cemetery
The cemetery is behind the church on Rue du Cimetière. The two men from 9/DLI are to be found in the far right hand corner of the cemetery, both were killed on 26 May during the heavy shelling of D Company in Provin.

Meuchin Churchyard

This is a large communal cemetery, which includes a German War Cemetery, and can be found on Rue de Pasteur. The single Second World War headstone is at the rear of the church and marks the spot where 26-year-old **Second Lieutenant Alfred Baines** of the 2/Essex is buried. Killed on 23 May, he was born in Wisbech, Cambridgeshire and married to Doris Baines. He initially joined the Honourable Artillery Company but transferred to the Essex Regiment in October 1939.

Carvin Communal Cemetery

This is another large communal cemetery with several entrances and can be found in the north-west corner of the town. To visit the CWGC Second World War plot the best entrance is at the junction of Rue de l'Égalité with Rue Victor Hugo, there is parking near the entrance. From the entrance walk up the main avenue for approximately 170 yards and turn left, the graves are close to the perimeter hedge near the German cemetery. A second plot, containing First World War graves, is close to the fence on Rue de l'Égalité. There are now over forty graves from the First World War and over thirty from the Second World War, a small number of which are unidentified. This is the last resting place of the 2/5 Leicesters who defended the Deûle Canal on 25 and 26 May against the might of the German 20th (Motorized) Division, although there are six men from 8/DLI also buried here. 22-year-old **Second Lieutenant Hugh Pope** (II.H.2) was serving with HQ Company when he was killed on 27 May. He joined the Leicesters in January 1940 and died almost immediately after being hit. **Second Lieutenant Charlie Hughes** (II.H.6) was a little older, at 39-years, and had been commissioned prior to embarking for France. Serving as the Leicester's Transport Officer, he was killed on 27 May. 21-year-old **Lance Corporal Harold Frost** (II.E.3) died of his wounds in captivity while **Lance Corporal Ken Hughes** (II.G.9) died in the same incident as Charlie Hughes. The men of 8/DLI were probably fighting with Second Lieutenant English's Carrier Platoon, who were in action against the advanced German units who had crossed the canal, although 23-year-old **Private Fred Bates** (II.G.4) remains a mystery, as the battalion was in action south west of Arras on 21 May and nowhere near Carvin.

Walk 1

The Bader Route at St-Omer

Start: Rue St-Bertin
Finish: Rue St-Bertin
Distance: Two and a half miles

I have not included a map for this walk as an excellent street plan can be obtained from the Tourist Office in Place Victor Hugo – tourisme-saintomer.com. Alternatively, you may wish to invest in the IGN Plan de Ville St-Omer, which also includes Arques. This circular walk begins outside the former **Clinique Sterin** in Rue St-Bertin, where the legless Wing Commander Douglas Bader was held in 1941, and follows his escape route to 129 Quai du Haut Pont. Rue St-Bertin is well worth further exploration, flanked as it is by the ruined Abbaye de St-Bertin to the east and the Cathedral de Notre Dame on its western end. From Quai du Haut Pont we return via the Qaui des Salines to Rue Carnot, where Field Marshal Lord Roberts died in 1914, before returning to Rue St-Bertin and the 1914-1918 GHQ building at Number 37.

Douglas Bader was shot down near St-Omer on 9 August 1941 while flying a Spitfire Vb with 616 Squadron during Circus 68. Of the eight aircraft shot down that day, four pilots were killed, four others were taken prisoner and one evaded captivity, escaping across the Pyrenees. Two of the dead are at Longuenesse Souvenir Cemetery; 19-year-old **Sergeant Gerald Haydon** (9.C.20), from 452 Squadron, and 27-year-old **Pilot Officer Douglas Waldon** (9.C.22), from 403 Squadron, are buried behind the Cross of Sacrifice.

Bader, having lost one of his legs while baling out of his aircraft, was taken to the Clinique Sterin on Rue St-Bertin, which has now been converted into flats. This post war development has altered the design of the rear of the property, where Bader climbed down knotted sheets to the ground, to the extent that little of the August 1941 layout remains. Now in possession of a new tin leg, Bader reached the ground and squeezed through the gates. Finding himself on Rue St-Bertin, a lighted cigarette indicated the presence of his guide, standing on the corner of **Rue du Tambour**:

177

The Clinique Sterin in Rue St-Bertin.

He stumped diagonally across the road and the cigarette moved, converging on him. It came to his side with a dark shadow behind it that whispered urgently 'Dooglass' in a strong French accent ... The shape took his right arm and they moved off along the pave. The town was like a tomb in which his legs were making an unholy clatter, echoing into the darkness.

Walk up Rue du Tambour into **Place St-Jean**, walking diagonally left past the Salle de Concert to reach **Rue de Monsigny**. The Salle de Concert , built by Pierre-Bernard Lefranc in 1834, is one of the oldest schools of music in France but it is unlikely Bader was in the mood for a visit! Turn left for some forty yards and walk up **Rue de l'Oeil** on the right to reach the wide **Rue Carnot**, where a zebra crossing will take you across the street. Turn left here for a few yards and then right along **Rue Gillaume Cliton**. Bader's account is unclear as to where he and his guide began to giggle, but it may have been in this area, their loud laughter 'mingled with the terror inside him that the Germans would hear'. Rue Gillaume Cliton is approximately 200 yards long, which for Bader must have seemed endless, as his right stump, devoid of its stump sock, began to chafe, causing him considerable pain and discomfort. At the junction with **Rue de Dunkerque** turn right for a few yards and then turn left into **Rue Hendricq**. By this time Bader must have been limping badly:

> *The steel leg had rubbed the skin off his groin and every step was searing agony. Stumbling and exhausted, he had both arms hanging on to the Frenchman's shoulders. At last the man took his arms around his neck, picked him up, dangling on his back and staggered along.*

Continue along Rue Hendricq for another eighty yards and turn right into **Rue du Soleil**, passing the block of flats named **Residence D Bader** on the right. Cross over Rue Edouard Devaux into **Rue du Bon Mariage** to reach **Boulevard de Strasbourg**. Cross straight over the road and bear right to walk over the level crossing. You are now walking alongside the canal and the road ahead of you is **Quai du Haut Pont**. Bader would have been carried up this road for another 500 yards before the two men turned left at the fork in the road along **Rue de la Faïencerie** to avoid the risk of being seen during the curfew. He entered **129 Quai du Haut Pont** via the rear entrance, where he was welcomed by the owners of the house:

> *An old man and a woman in a black shawl got up from the chairs and the woman put her arms round him and kissed him. She was over sixty, Madame Hiècque, plump and with a lined patient face. Her husband, spare and stooping, brushed his cheeks with a wisp of grey moustache.*

The level crossing over which Douglas Bader would have been carried by his guide.

The fork in the road with Rue de la Faiencerie to the left and Quai du Haut Pont to the right.

129 Quai du Haut Pont.

For a better frontal view of the house, continue alongside the canal; the house is a small terrace with a brick facade and a single downstairs window. Bader was betrayed by one of the clinique staff and was discovered hiding in the garden shed by a German search party.

Retrace your steps along Quai du Haut Pont to the level crossing and walk along **Rue de Metz** to the roundabout. Directly opposite, on the left of a waterway, you will see **Quai des Salines**. Follow this road round to the left and take the second bridge – Rue de Cassel – which crosses the waterway on your right. At the junction with **Rue Robert le Frison** turn left then immediately right into **Rue de l'Arbalère** which leads, after 200 yards, to the junction with **Rue Gillaume Cliton**. You will recognize this

The Quai des Salines is on the right and runs alongside an attractive waterway.

intersection from Bader's walk. Turn left and then right into **Rue Carnot**. The building where Lord Roberts died on 14 November 1914 – 52 Rue Carnot – is 185 yards further along the street on the right hand side: a blue plaque marks the building. The 82-year-old Field Marshal Lord Roberts was appointed Commander-in-Chief of overseas troops in France in August 1914 and spent much of 11 November – a bitterly cold day – at the Longuenesse Airfield, followed by another gruelling day on 12 November inspecting troops and visiting various army headquarters. The next day was no different and Roberts was at Cassel

The Blue Plaque marking the house where Field Marshal Lord Roberts died in 1914.

and Bailleul before scrambling up the Sherpenberg in an attempt to see the shelling at Ypres. This level of activity and the adverse weather conditions were obviously too much for the ageing Field Marshal and he died the next evening.

Almost opposite 52 Rue Carnot is the narrow **Rue St-Denis**, a street that leads to **Place St-Denis** and its church. After walking past the church and into Rue St-Bertin, find the facade of Number 37, which was the building that housed BEF GHQ during 1914–March 1916. The house opposite was where George V stayed when he visited St-Omer. From here it is now only a few yards back to where you parked your vehicle.

No. 137 Rue St-Bertin, which housed the Headquarters of the BEF between October 1914–March 1916.

Walk 2

Gorre

Start: The car park on Rue Jules Bailleul
Finish: The car park on Rue Jules Bailleul
Distance: Two miles (four miles if Beuvry Communal Cemetery and
                Extension are included)
Map: IGN 1:25,000 Lens 2405E

This short circular walk begins at the car park – **Plas du 19 Mars 1962** – in the main street of Gorre. The 19 May 1962 marked the cease fire in the French Algerian War, which had lasted for nearly eight years. The walk takes in the D Company, 1/RIF, positions which the battalion held from 21 until 26 May, after which they were relieved by 1/8 Lancashire Fusiliers. We also visit the site of the former **château at Gorre** before

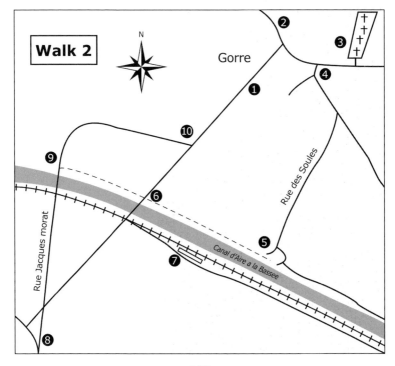

183

The entrance gates to the former château at Gorre.

heading east to the **British and Indian Cemetery**. On returning to the canal there is a good view of the former railway goods yard on the far bank, from where 17 Platoon, 1/RIF, watched the destruction of a French ammunition train on 25 May. After crossing the canal over the footbridge we walk south to the **Beuvry Memorial** to the French civilian victims of the Second World War before heading north again to cross the canal over the Lens Bridge.

After leaving the car park ❶ in Plas du 19 Mars 1962, turn right and walk up Rue Jules Bailleul to where the road bends sharply round to the right; on your left is a minor road, which led past the former château, For much of the First World War, the château stood behind a section of the British front line that ran northward along the Aubers Ridge from Givenchy-lès-La-Bassée to Festubert. From the end of the Battle of Festubert in May 1915 until the spring of 1918 this was considered to be a relatively quiet sector. The village of Gorre was occasionally bombarded by German artillery during this period but the château remained intact and its rooms were used as an officers' mess and headquarters for British units stationed in the area. ❷ The grounds of the château were also the site of several artillery emplacements, a rifle range,

184

an improvised parade ground and football pitch. Throughout 1916 and 1917 British troops could be seen drilling in the fields next to the château or unloading supplies from barges on the canal.

At the junction you will see a CWGC signpost directing you to **Gorre British and Indian Cemetery**; follow this sign to the cemetery, which you will see on your left. ❸ The cemetery is located in the south-east corner of the original château grounds and was begun in the autumn of 1914. The Indian section of the cemetery was closed in October 1915 but the British section was used by infantry and artillery units stationed in the area until April 1918, when the relative quiet of the sector was shattered by the German Spring Offensive and Gorre became a support post close behind the front line during the Battle of Estaire. This battle was one of two massive German assaults of the BEF's positions from Ypres to Festubert that became known as the Battles of the Lys. When the battle began on 9 April, the 55th (West Lancashire) Division occupied the frontline trenches running north from Givenchy to Richebourg L'Avoué. The Allied positions to their left, around the village of le Touret, were held by Portuguese units. After a preliminary artillery bombardment that began on the evening of 7 April, the German Sixth Army, spearheaded by storm troops, attacked in force early on the morning of 9 April. Heavy mist enabled the attackers to get very close to the Allied

Gorre British and Indian Cemetery.

lines before they were observed and Portuguese units suffered heavy casualties and began to retire. Further south, the various formations of the 55th Division were hard pressed from the outset and the front line trenches around Givenchy were the scene of fierce fighting between British and German troops. The divisional brigade holding the northern section of the British line was forced to pull back, but well organized counter-attacks and determined defence elsewhere enabled the 55th Division to hold its ground and prevent a major German breakthrough. Fighting continued in the trenches east of Gorre until 17 April when the German forces finally broke off the attack. In just over a week of fighting almost 3,000 officers and men of the division had been killed, wounded, or taken prisoner, but the territory over which they had fought remained in Allied hands.

After the German advance across the canal in May 1940, it was the 1/8 Lancashire Fusiliers that bore the brunt of the fighting and, as part of the battalion withdrew up through Gorre, the cemetery was prepared for defence. As you move amongst the headstones take note of the number of Lancashire men who rest here and ponder for a moment the scene in May 1940 when the 1/8 Lancashire Fusiliers, surrounded by the dead of the 55th (West Lancashire) Division, fought again to hold a German advance amongst the ghosts of their fathers and uncles. Before you leave the cemetery note the shrapnel marks that are still in existence on the entrance gate and other structures, the only remaining visible legacy from the Second World War.

Now walk back towards Gorre and take the first turning ❹ on the left – Rue des Chantieres. After 150 yards turn right onto Rue des Saules and walk down to the canal, turning right ❺ onto the towpath. After a few yards stop and look across the canal to the railway halt. You are now standing in the positions occupied by **Second Lieutenant Desmond Gethin** and the men of 17 Platoon, 1/RIF. In May 1940 the area occupied by the railway halt and car park was a railway goods yard with numerous sidings. For some time 17 Platoon had been bothered by German snipers firing at them from the cover of the railway lines and wagons of a French ammunition train which had been left in the siding. Gethin's Company Commander, **Lieutenant John Horsfall**, described the ensuing explosion that took place on 25 May:

Desmond Gethin's problem was solved for him in the end without further action on 17's part, and the ensuing drama, like so many other incidents, would not be forgotten by the defenders of Gorre in 1940. ... Of course we had by then forgotten the contents of the ammunition wagons, but eventually the inevitable happened, and

The canal side locations of 17 Platoon, 1/RIF, together with moored barges.

touched off either by one of our own shells or perhaps one of the [German] aircraft's bombs, there was a chain reaction of explosions like that of the Ninove bridge going up, but multiplied several times over. That same soundless but cataclysmic shock, this time in series, which made one gasp and which never seemed to end, but when it finally did, brought all to cessation – save for the fragments and ragments which dropped from the sky like hail over the whole battlefield.

Nothing remained of the goods yard or, as Horsfall was pleased to report, of the German garrison, and for a long time afterwards the whole scene was shrouded in a thick fog.

Walk alongside the canal until you reach the footbridge ❻ – Passerelle de Beuvry – cross the canal and railway line and descend into **Rue Georges Clemenceau**, where an ornamental garden has been constructed in the former goods yard. ❼ The railway halt and car park can be seen beyond.

The footbridge across the canal connecting Gorre with Beuvry.

Looking up Rue Jean Lefebure towards the footbridge from the Beuvry Memorial.

Continue down Rue Jean Lefebure to the road junction, bearing left to the memorial to the French civilians of Beuvry ❽ who were victims of the Second World War, which is flanked by two smaller memorials: one commemorates the centenary of the 1848 Revolution, while the other is a permanent memorial to **Sous Lieutenant Jacques Morat**, who was killed on 24 May 1940. **Beuvry Communal Cemetery and Extension** is one mile further south along **Rue Léon Callot**; you can either walk down to the cemetery or visit it later after you have returned to the car park on Rue Jules Bailleul.

From the memorial retrace your steps along **Rue Jacques Morat,** which takes its name from the memorial, and, ignoring the junction on the right leading back to the footbridge, walk straight ahead to the main bridge over the canal. This is **Pont de Gorre** or the Lens bridge, ❾ as described by Lieutenant John Horsfall, and should be crossed on the right hand side where a set of steep steps leads down to the towpath. Walk

The Beuvry Memorial.

188

The modern day Pont de Gorre was described by John Horsfall as the Lens Bridge.

along the canal towpath to the footbridge and turn left past a building on the right marked **Brassiere de Pont de Gorre**. The next roundabout ⑩ is the approximate location of the D Company, 1/RIF, Headquarters, and while there are one or two buildings that are likely contenders for Horsfall's HQ, it has proved impossible to pinpoint with any accuracy exactly which one. From the roundabout it is only another 250 yards back to your vehicle in Plas du 19 Mars 1962.

Cemeteries
Beuvry Communal Cemetery and Extension
The main entrance is on **Rue Eduard Vaillant**, where there is parking. This is a large communal cemetery with five separate CWGC plots dotted around the cemetery. In the main cemetery near the extension there is a row of thirty-three 1940 headstones, one of which is unidentified. These men are mainly from the 1/8 Lancashire Fusiliers and 2/Dorsets who fought in and around Gorre. 24-year-old **Second Lieutenant Henry Braddyll** (Grave 97) was serving with 5/Field Company when he was killed on 27 May. **Wing Commander John Llewelyn** (Grave 54A) was the squadron commander of 40 Squadron and flying a Blenheim IV on 23 May when his aircraft was hit by flak and crashed near Beuvry. **Pilot Officer William Edwards** was also killed and is buried at Sailly-Labourse Communal Cemetery. The third crew member, **Sergeant Beattie**, later returned safely to the squadron.

The extension to the communal cemetery is marked by the cross of sacrifice; here there are a row of 1940 burials on either side of the cross and it would appear that casualties were brought in from the surrounding battlefields as there is a mixture of units represented here. 41-year-old **Lieutenant Edward Smith** (1.B.7) was awarded the Victoria Cross in

October 1918 after taking command of his platoon and leading them in an astonishing crusade against several enemy machine gun positions. Re-enlisting in the 2/Lancashire Fusiliers, he died before the German invasion on 12 January 1940, possibly from a friendly fire incident. His headstone is marked by the motif of the Victoria Cross. The accidental detonation of an anti-tank mine on 16 December 1939 was responsible for the death of 20-year-old **Second Lieutenant Peter Milward** (1.B.2) of the 2/Duke of Cornwall's Light Infantry. The explosion killed the Royal Engineers instructor and nine pupils, including **Second Lieutenant Michael Arnold** (1.B.1) and 25-year-old **Second Lieutenant Richard Mitchell** (1.B.6) of the 2/Lincolnshires. It is likely that 24-year-old **Lieutenant Basil Reiss** (1.B.4), Royal Engineers, and **Lieutenant Harold Hull** (1.B.3), 2/Lancashire Fusiliers, were also killed in the explosion.

Nearby Cemeteries
Béthune Town Cemetery
This is a large communal cemetery and can be found from almost any point in Béthune by following signposts for *Cimetière Nord*. Satnav users may find it useful to find Rue du Pont de Pierres, which will take you straight to the car park. Walk straight up the main avenue towards the top of the cemetery, from where the Cross of Sacrifice will become visible. The cemetery contains 3,004 burials from the First World War, eleven of which remain unidentified, and nineteen Second World War burials, of whom two are unidentified. In addition, visitors will find 122 French graves and eighty-seven German graves.

As you approach the CWGC shelter and the War Stone you will pass the first of the British graves on the right. Here you will find the grave of 27-year-old **Lieutenant Frank de Pass VC** (1.A.24), a schoolboy friend of Rupert Brooke at Rugby School. De Pass was awarded the Victoria Cross on 24 November 1914 while serving with the 34/Poona Horse, near Festubert. He was the thirty-seventh recipient of the Victoria Cross on the Western Front during the First World War.

The Second World War headstones are clustered around the central shelter and the War Stone and here you will find 21-year-old **Second Lieutenant John Raine** (3.LL.10), who was serving with the 2/Dorsets and died of wounds during the night of 27 May. It is likely he died during his battalion's withdrawal to Festubert and he is also commemorated on his parent's gravestone in Darlington West Cemetery. Apart from the four men who were killed in 1944, the dates of death on most of the remaining 1940 graves suggest they are men who died locally of wounds whilst in captivity.

Walk 3

The Massacre at Louis Creton's Farm

Start: The church at Paradis
Finish: Le Paradis War Cemetery
Distance: Two miles
Map: IGN 1:25,000 Hazebrouck 2404O

The village of Paradis is north of Locon on the D178. This is quite an emotive walk as you are treading in the footsteps of the officers and men who were being marched to their deaths. Park your vehicle outside the church at Paradis, ❶ where a monument has been erected to the ninety seven men who were murdered on 27 May at Louis Creton's farm. The war cemetery is an extension of the churchyard and can either be visited

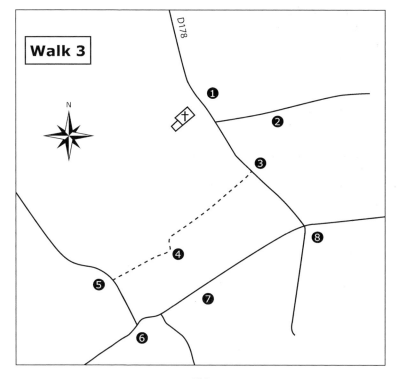

The memorial outside the church commemorating the ninety-seven murdered men.

before you begin the walk or afterwards. Before you leave the church look up the road towards Merville, **Lieutenant Colonel Money** was evidently concerned at the possibility of being attacked from the rear and established three posts further along on the road to cover this eventuality with Captain Mackinnon's B Company deployed along Rue de Cerisiers.

Keeping the church on your right, walk down the main street for eighty-five yards and turn left along **Rue de Derrière**. At this road junction Money placed four section posts, each equipped with a Boys rifle, along with Major Rodney Watson's D Company, who were astride the road leading up from the canal. Watson was killed shortly afterwards. It was a little further along this road that Money established the Royal Scot's Battalion HQ and the RAP. Exactly where it was situated is shrouded amongst the post-war building, but we do know it was located in a farm, the first of which you will find on the right after 380 yards. Whether this was the site of ❷ Money's HQ is anyone's guess, but it is unlikely that he would have wanted to be situated any further from the action. The RAP was of course one of the first places to be overwhelmed by the Germans as their forces approached the village from the east and where the medical officer and the battalion padre, **Padre MacLean**, argued with an SS NCO who wanted to shoot the wounded! It is interesting to note that several of the RAP orderlies later escaped from the building.

Retrace your steps to the main road and turn left. The main street was where Lieutenant Colonel Money was wounded by shellfire and returned to the RAP before being transported to La Gorgue Dressing Station. The speed of the German advance on both sides of the village was illustrated by the fact that the vehicle that was transporting him had to rush an enemy presence on the road south of La Gorgue.

Immediately before a small bridge turn right, this is the ❸ **Chemin Vasseur**, which soon gives way to a grass track. You are now walking

Chemin Vasseur.

parallel with the Chemin du Paradis and across to your left should be able to make out the tall buildings of **Duries Farm**, which was the Norfolk's HQ. In 450 yards, just after the track bends to the left, you will come to the rear ❹ of Duries Farm. Although there is a ditch running alongside the track, in May 1940 there was probably an access path that connected **Duries Farm** with the track you are now standing on. It was at this point

The field at the rear of Duries Farm, across which Major Ryder and his men were marched.

that the surrendering men of the Norfolk's HQ Company were herded out of the farm buildings and collected in the field to the right of the track, along with other prisoners who had been captured previously. Standing with the Norfolks were men from the Royal Scots, Royal Artillery, Manchester Regiment and, it is said, one French soldier.

It was probably in this field that the fate of the prisoners was discussed. The German soldiers were members of the 1st Battalion of the SS-*Totenkopf's* 2nd Infantry Regiment and there is plenty of evidence regarding the brutality of the German soldiers towards the prisoners while they were in the field, although it is not known whether this occurred before or after the fate of the prisoners had been decided. Walk on to the junction of the ❺ track with **Rue du Perret**, you are now walking in the footsteps of the men who were about to be massacred. Turn left and walk on down **Rue du Perret** to the junction with Chemin du Paradis. At the junction the buildings that were **Louis Creton's Farm** in 1940 can be seen almost straight ahead. Turn right and walk across to

Looking down Rue du Perret towards the buildings of Louis Creton's Farm.

The memorial stone at Louis Creton's Farm.

the memorial stone that you can see to the right of a metalled gate. Erected in May 1990 the memorial marks the field in which the ninety-nine prisoners were marched and lined up against the wall of the barn on the left. ❻ The barn now has a memorial stone set into the wall as a permanent reminder of what took place here. If you wish to go into the field, the present owner of the farm is only too willing to unlock the gate. Before you do, be reminded of the words of **Private Albert Pooley**, a Norfolk man serving with A Company, who was one of only two men to survive the massacre:

> *Before I turned into that gateway, I saw with one of the nastiest feelings I've ever had in my life, two heavy machine-guns inside the meadow. They were manned and pointing at the head of our column! I felt as though an icy hand had gripped my stomach. The guns began to spit fire and even as the front men began to fall I said fiercely, 'This can't be. They can't do this to us!' For a few seconds the cries and shrieks of our stricken men drowned the cracking of the guns. Men fell like grass before a scythe. The invisible blade came nearer and then swept through me. I felt a terrific searing pain in my leg and wrist and pitched forward engulfed in a red world of tearing agony. My scream of pain mingled with the cries of my mates but even as I fell forward into a heap of dying men the thought stabbed my brain, 'If I ever get out of here the swine who did this will pay for it'.*

After the machine gun fire stopped the prisoners that still showed signs of life were either bayoneted or shot; but miraculously two managed to remain alive. **Privates Pooley** and **William O'Callaghan**, although badly wounded, finally extricated themselves from the pile of corpses

Ninety-nine men were lined up in front of this barn and machine-gunned.

195

CETTE PLAQUE COMMEMORE LES QUATRE VINGT DIX SEPT SOLDATS
DU ROYAL NORFOLK ET D'AUTRES REGIMENTS
QUI FURENT MASSACRES A CET ENDROIT LE 27 MAI 1940

QUE LEUR SACRIFICE NE SOIT PAS VAIN

THIS PLAQUE COMMEMORATES THE NINETY SEVEN ALL RANKS
OF THE ROYAL NORFOLK AND OTHER REGIMENTS
WHO WERE MASSACRED AT THIS SPOT ON 27TH MAY 1940

MAY THEIR SACRIFICE BE NOT IN VAIN

A plaque is now set into the wall of the barn as a constant reminder of the horrific crime that was committed here.

which had once been their comrades and struggled across the fields to a nearby farm — now the Duquenne Transport Company – where Madam Duquenne and her son tended to their wounds. They were eventually taken prisoner by the Wehrmacht.

From the farm turn right and walk along the Chemin du Paradis towards the village for approximately 200 yards and stop outside Duries Farm, which you can see on the left. ❼ These were the buildings where **Major Ryder** and the men of HQ Company were positioned. If you walk round to the rear of the building and peer through the post-war metal barn, you can see the numerous outbuildings that housed the company signallers and gives you some impression of the extent of them. Walk round to the front of the farm house, where **Signaller Robert Brown** and

The farm house at Duries Farm.

Captain Charles Long took the decision to exit via the front door rather than follow Major Ryder out to the rear of the farm, a decision that saved their lives.

Walk on past Duries Farm, which marked the approximate boundary between the German 1st and 2nd SS Battalions of the 2nd Infantry Regiment, and on reaching the main road turn left. ❽ You are now back in the main street of the village and will pass **Chemin Vasseur** on your left before reaching your vehicle by the church. This is a good moment to visit the cemetery.

Cemeteries
Le Paradis War Cemetery

The entrance can be found at the end of the passageway to the right of the church. There are now over 150 men from the Second World War commemorated on this site but sadly nearly a third remain unidentified, a sad reflection of the chaos that was prevalent in France at the time and the degree of decomposition that had overtaken a number of the bodies murdered at Louis Creton's farm. There is still no official roll of honour to accompany the massacre; one possible reason is the degree of uncertainty as to who exactly was executed by the SS. The dead at the farm were buried soon afterwards in the field where they lay and it was not until 1942 that the bodies were exhumed and reinterred at the churchyard in Paradis – now the site of Le Paradis War Cemetery. However, we do know that the Mayor of Béthune reported details of the

Le Paradis War Cemetery.

massacre to the Allied authorities in October 1944, and in his report stated that ninety-seven soldiers – temporarily buried at the massacre site until 1942, were re-interred at Le Paradis War Cemetery, providing a list of forty-five identified bodies. All of this leaves a large question mark over the level of disbelief that greeted Pooley and O'Callaghan when they first reported the massacre to the authorities in England.

Buried here are sixty-one identified officers and men of the Royal Norfolks, including their commanding officer, 38-year-old **Major Lisle Ryder** (1.G.1). Not all of these were victims of the massacre, as a number were killed during the German bombing attack on Beuvry on 10 May and in the subsequent fighting south of Paradis. Of the thirty-four officers and men of the Royal Scots, the most senior is 36-year-old **Major Rodney Watson** (1.B.9), who commanded D Company and was killed on 27 May. Four other Royal Scots were killed on 27 May; but that does not necessarily mean that they were victims of the massacre. What is more disturbing is the number of unidentified burials, of which the vast majority must be victims of the massacre and were too badly decomposed to be identified when they were reinterred in 1942.

The RAF casualties are all from a 44 Squadron Hampden 1 from Waddington, which was shot down north of Béthune after bombing rail targets on the night of 12 June 1940, highlighting the continuation of the air war that carried on after the BEF had been evacuated from Dunkerque. The pilot, 26-Year-old **Flight Sergeant Cyril Sumster** (2.A.6) and his three crew, 27-year-old **Sergeant William Jeffrey** (2.A.7), 28-year-old **Sergeant Jack Sandall** (2.A.6) and 25-year-old **Sergeant James Simpson** (2.A.5), were all killed.

Selected Bibliography

The National Archives
Unit War Diaries in WO 166 and 167.
Personal accounts in CAB 106 and WO 217.
POW Reports in WO 344, WO 373.

Imperial War Museum Sound Archive
Imperial War Museum Department of Documents
The National Army Museum
The RUSI Library

Published Sources
Baxter, I, *Blitzkrieg in the West*, Pen and Sword 2010
Bishop, T, *One Young Soldier*, Michael Russell 1993
Blaxland, G, *Destination Dunkirk: The Story of Gort's Army*, William
    Kimber 1973
Blight, G, *The History of The Royal Berkshire Regiment 1920-1947*,
    Staples 1953
Boardman, C J, *Tracks in Europe*, Royal Inniskilling Dragoon Guards
    1990
Dildy, D.C, *Fall Gelb 1940 (1)*, Osprey 2014
Ellis, L.F, *The War in France and Flanders*, HMSO 1953
Farndale, M, *History of the Royal Regiment of Artillery*, Brasseys 1996
Foster, R, The *History of the Queen's Royal Regiment, Volume VIII
    1924-1948*, Gale and Polden 1953
Frieser, K-H, *The Blitzkrieg Legend*, Naval Institute Press 2012
Gough, G F, *Thirty Days To Dunkirk*, Bridge Books 1990
Guderian, H, *Panzer Leader*, Michael Joseph 1952
Hart, L, *The Rommel Papers*, Collins 1953
Horsfall, J, *Say Not the Struggle*, Roundwood Press 1977
Jackson, J, *The Fall of France,* OUP 2003
Lynch, T, *Dunkirk 1940 'Whereabouts Unknown'*, History Press 2010
Kemp, P.K, *The Red Dragon. The Story of the Royal Welch Fusiliers
    1919-1945*, Gale and Polden 1960
Muir, A, *The First Of Foot*, The Royal Scots 1961
Murland, J. D, *Retreat and Rearguard: Dunkirk 1940*, Pen and Sword
    2015
Philson, A, *The British Army 1939-1945 Organization and Order of
    Battle Volume 6*, Military Press 2007

Richardson, M, *Tigers at Dunkirk*, Pen and Sword 2010

Rissik, D, *The DLI at War*, N&M Reprint

Rodgers, G, *In Search of Tom*, Cormorant 2009

Sebag-Montefiore, H, *Dunkirk – Fight to the Last Man*, Viking 2006

Synge, W, *The Story of the Green Howards*, The Regiment 1954

Underhill, W, *The History of The Royal Leicestershire Regiment*, Rowe 1957

Usher, K, *Charles 'Dougie' Usher*, Createspace 2014

White, G, *Straight on for Tokyo, The War History of the 2nd Battalion Dorsetshire Regiment*, Gale and Polden 1948

Younger, T, *Blowing Our Bridges*, Pen and Sword 2004

Index

Hitler Halt Order, vii, 6–10, 79, 81, 133

Holque, bridge at, 27, 132

Horsbrugh-Porter, Maj A., 43–4

Horsfall, Lt J., 57, 60–2, 110, 186–9

Hoth, H., 10, 12

Irwin, 2/Lt A., 65–7

Isbergues, 10, 12, 49–50, 160

Johnson, Capt J., 83, 88

Kleist, P. von, 10–11

Knoechlein, F., 105–107

La Bassée, x, xii, 9, 37, 55, 63–4, 77, 79, 113–14, 117, 121–2, 168, 172

Lawson's Force, 53–4

Leah, Capt R., 117–20

Le Cochon Noir, 24–6, 126–7, 129

Les Targette, bridge at, 17–20, 23, 131–2

Lloyd, Maj I., 44, 144

Longuenesse airfield, 141, 181

Louis Creton's Farm, 13, 104–106, 191, 194–7

Macforce, 10, 37–8, 48

Mardyck, Canal, 24

Mardyck, Fort, 23

McLane, Sgt M., 89, 94, 162

Merville, xii, 30, 48, 100–102, 151, 192

Money, Lt Col H., 100–103, 192, 193

Morel, Cap C., 21, 24–5

O'Callaghan, W., 106–107, 195, 198

Polforce, 10, 15, 33, 37–54, 68, 81

Pont Fixe, 56–7, 110, 168, 170

Parkes, Lt Col J., 114–16

Payne, 2/Lt K., 47–8, 145

Petch, Maj L., 22, 25

Pilleau, Lt Col G., 62–3

Pooley, A., 105–107, 195, 198

Pont-à-Vendin, 12, 65, 70–1, 76

Pulleyn, Lt Col E., 52

Reeves, Maj B., 20–3, 25, 127

Reinhardt, H., 11–12, 79

Renescure, 40–1, 144

Renescure, bridge at, 44–5, 143–4, 151

Robecq, 52–3, 79–83, 87–8, 94, 154, 160

Roberts, F/Marshall Lord, 177, 181–2

Rodgers, Pte T., 162–4

Rommel, E., 6, 8, 13, 61

Royal Welch Fusiliers Memorial, 157–9

Ruddle, Lt Col K., 68–1, 75–8

Rundstedt, G. von, vii,1, 7–10

Rustyforce, 10, 81

Ryder, Maj L., 97, 104–105, 193, 196–8

Salomé, 62, 64, 70, 117, 168, 172, 175

Sillar, Lt W., 108–109

Simpson, Lt Col R., 84–6, 88, 91–3, 156, 160–1

Stayner, Lt Col D., 107–108

Steel, Lt Col M., 19–20, 23–4

Stephenson, Lt Col E., 111–13, 168–9, 171

St-Floris, 82–3, 87, 154–6

St-Momelin, bridge at, 15, 29–32, 34, 36, 40–1, 96, 139